O'NEILL

in an hour

BY JAMES FISHER

WITHDRAWN

SUSAN C. MOORE, SERIES EDITOR

PLAYWRIGHTS in an hour

know the playwright, love the play

IN AN HOUR BOOKS • HANOVER, NEW HAMPSHIRE • INANHOURBOOKS.COM
AN IMPRINT OF SMITH AND KRAUS PUBLISHERS, INC • SMITHANDKRAUS.COM

With grateful thanks to Carl R. Mueller,
whose fascinating introductions to his translations of the Greek and
German playwrights provided inspiration for this series.

Published by In an Hour Books
an imprint of Smith and Kraus, Inc.
177 Lyme Road, Hanover, NH 03755
inanhourbooks.com SmithandKraus.com

Know the playwright, love the play.

In an Hour, In a Minute, and Theater IQ are registered trademarks of
In an Hour Books.

Excerpts printed in this book are from plays in the public domain.

Front cover design by Dan Mehling, dmehling@gmail.com
Text design by Kate Mueller, Electric Dragon Productions
Book production by Dede Cummings Design, DCDesign@sover.net

ISBN-13: 978-1-936232-05-5
ISBN-10: 1-936232-05-7
Library of Congress Control Number: 2009943217

CONTENTS

Why Playwrights in an Hour?

This new series by Smith and Kraus Publishers titled Playwrights in an Hour has a dual purpose for being; one academic, the other general. For the general reader, this volume, as well as the many others in the series, offers in compact form the information needed for a basic understanding and appreciation of the works of each volume's featured playwright. Which is not to say that there don't exist volumes on end devoted to each playwright under consideration. But inasmuch as few are blessed with enough time to read the splendid scholarship that is available, a brief, highly focused accounting of the playwright's life and work is in order.

The central feature of the series, a thirty- to forty-page essay, integrates the playwright into the context of his or her time and place. And the volumes, though written to high standards of academic integrity, are accessible in style and approach to the general reader as well as to the student, and of course to the theater professional and theatergoer.

These books will serve for the brushing up of one's knowledge of a playwright's career, to the benefit of theater work or theatergoing. The Playwrights in an Hour series represents all periods of Western theater: Aeschylus to Shakespeare to Wedekind to Ibsen to Williams to Beckett, and on to the great contemporary playwrights who continue to offer joy and enlightenment to a grateful world.

Carl R. Mueller
School of Theater, Film and Television
Department of Theater
University of California, Los Angeles

Introduction

E ugene O'Neill is unequivocally the greatest dramatist America
ever produced. Yet, his reputation will rest on his last plays, a
few of them produced only after his death.

A restless experimenter, and the first American to use European
theater techniques to explore provincial themes, O'Neill followed a
career arc very similar to that of his idol, August Strindberg. Using
masks, dopplegangers, soliloquies, and dream plays, he finally settled
into a realistic style like Henrik Ibsen's, focusing on what he called "the
family Kodak" — himself and his own benighted immediate relatives.

O'Neill's earlier plays are hardly without value. Indeed, they garnered him numerous Pulitzers and, in 1936, the Nobel Prize. Some, like
Desire Under the Elms (1924–1925), contain powerful scenes; others,
like *The Great God Brown* (1925–1926), have interesting themes; and
some, like those long endurance trips, *Mourning Becomes Electra*
(1931) and *Strange Interlude* (1928), are sustained by the sheer force of
the author's will. Still, the bulk of O'Neill's writings before his one comedy, *Ah Wilderness!* (1932–1933) in 1933, are like the groping prepara-
tory sketches of one who had to write badly in order to write well. No
major dramatist, with the possible exception of George Bernard Shaw,
has produced so many second-rate plays.

But with *The Iceman Cometh* (1939) and *Long Day's Journey Into
Night* (1939–1942) — and to a lesser extent with *Hughie* (1941) and *A
Moon for the Misbegotten* (1941–1943) — O'Neill developed from a self-
conscious stammering experimenter into an eloquent artist and poet,
concentrating a fierce bullish power into fables of reality and illusion.
Shot through with flashes of humor, they are yet pervaded by a sense of
melancholy over the human condition. The hiatus between *Ah Wilderness!* and *Days Without End* (1933), and *The Iceman Cometh* (written in
1939 but not produced until 1946), was the longest of his career. But in
this time lapse, something portentous was happening in O'Neill's life.

He was beginning to write about his family, uncovering painful secrets that hitherto had been shrouded in darkness. Instead of feeling superior to his subjects, he took his own condition as a metaphor for the cankered state of the nation. With these honest, remorseless probes into his own past in plays like *The Iceman Cometh, Hughie,* and especially, *Long Day's Journey Into Night,* O'Neill began to approach the Truth as he looked the Gorgon full in the face. It is for these last plays that he will be remembered — plays he wrote full of pain and suffering, a sick and tired man in a shuttered room, unable to bear much light.

In power and insight, O'Neill still remains unsurpassed among American dramatists. It is doubtful that there would have been an American drama without him.

Robert Brustein
Founding director of the Yale and American Repertory Theatres
Distinguished Scholar in Residence, Suffolk University
Senior Research Fellow, Harvard University

O'Neill

IN A MINUTE

AGE	YEAR	
–	1888	**Enter Eugene Gladstone O'Neill, October 16.**
1	1889	The Moulin Rouge opens in Paris.
4	1892	General Electric is established.
7	1895	Oscar Wilde — *The Importance of Being Earnest*
9	1897	J. J. Thomson discovers the electron.
12	1900	The first automobile show is held in New York City.
13	1901	Teddy Roosevelt inaugurated. Says: "Speak softly and carry a big stick."
16	1904	J. M. Barrie — *Peter Pan, or The Boy Who Wouldn't Grow Up*
19	1907	John M. Synge — *Playboy of the Western World*
21	1909	Robert Peary reaches the North Pole.
22	1910	Vatican orders all priests to take oath against modernism.
29	1917	Lenin orders execution of Czar Nicolas II and family, ending 300 years of Romanov rule.
30	1918	Germany is defeated, ending The Great War.
32	**1920**	**Eugene O'Neill — *Emperor Jones***
33	**1921**	**Eugene O'Neill — *"Anna Christie"***
34	1922	Michael Collins is assassinated during Irish Civil War.
36	**1924**	**Eugene O'Neill — *Desire Under the Elms* written**
39	**1927**	**Eugene O'Neill — *Strange Interlude* written**
40	1928	Mickey Mouse and Minnie Mouse debut in Walt Disney films.
41	1929	William Faulkner — *The Sound and the Fury*
43	**1931**	**Eugene O'Neill — *Mourning Becomes Electra* written**
44	**1932**	**Eugene O'Neill — *Ah, Wilderness!* written**
47	1935	Alcoholics Anonymous (AA) is founded.
49	1937	Disney — *Snow White and the Seven Dwarfs*
50	1938	Thornton Wilder — Our Town
53	**1941**	**Eugene O'Neill — *Long Day's Journey Into Night* written**
57	1945	GIs liberate inmates of Nazi extermination camps.
58	**1946**	**Eugene O'Neill — *The Iceman Cometh***
65	**1953**	**Exit Eugene Gladstone O'Neill, November 27.**
–	1957	**Eugene O'Neill — *Long Day's Journey Into Night***

A snapshot of the playwright's world. From historical events to pop-culture and the literary landscape of the time, this brief list catalogues events that directly or indirectly impacted the playwright's writing. Play citations refer to opening or premiere dates, unless otherwise noted.

O'Neill

HIS WORKS

ONE-ACT PLAYS

A Wife for Life (vaudeville sketch)

The Web

Thirst

Recklessness

Warnings

Fog

Bound East for Cardiff

Abortion

The Movie Man

The Sniper

Before Breakfast

Ile

The Long Voyage Home

In the Zone

The Moon of the Caribbees

The Rope

The Dreamy Kid

Where the Cross Is Made

Shell Shock

Hughie

PLAYS

Bread and Butter

Servitude

The Personal Equation

This section presents a complete list of the playwright's works in chronological order by date written.

ESSAYS

O'Neill published three essays, "Memoranda on Masks," "Second
Thoughts," and "A Dramatist's Notebook," in *The American
Spectator* between November 1932 and January 1933.

POETRY

A collection of Eugene O'Neill's poetry was published in 1980. See Eugene O'Neill. *Poems: 1912–1944*. Edited with introduction by Donald Gallup. New Haven & New York: Ticknor and Fields, 1980.

SHORT STORY

"Tomorrow" (1917) is included in *Eugene O'Neill: Complete Plays 1932–1943*. New York: Library of America, 1988.

Onstage with O'Neill

*Introducing Colleagues and
Contemporaries of Eugene O'Neill*

 THEATER

George Abbott, American playwright, director, and actor

Maxwell Anderson, American playwright

Robert Benchley, American writer and actor

Irving Berlin, American songwriter

Lynn Fontanne, English actress

Al Jolson, Lithuanian-American entertainer and singer

George S. Kaufman, American playwright and director

Ed Wynn, American actor and entertainer

 ARTS

Thomas Hart Benton, American painter

Marc Chagall, Russian artist

Jelly Roll Morton, American jazz musician and composer

Georgia O'Keeffe, American painter

Man Ray, American photographer

Diego Rivera, Mexican painter

Ludwig Mies van der Rohe, German architect

Egon Schiele, Austrian painter

This section lists contemporaries whom the playwright may or may not have known.

FILM
Roscoe "Fatty" Arbuckle, American actor and director
Charlie Chaplin, English actor and director
Abel Gance, French filmmaker
Jean Hersholt, Danish actor
Fritz Lang, Austrian filmmaker
Stan Laurel, English actor
The Marx Brothers (Groucho, Harpo, Chico, Zeppo, Gummo),
    American actors
James Whale, English filmmaker

POLITICS/MILITARY
David Ben-Gurion, prime minister of Israel
Michael Collins, Irish nationalist and activist
Dwight D. Eisenhower, World War II general and president of the
    United States
Marcus Garvey, Jamaican Pan-African black-nationalist activist
Charles de Gaulle, French general and president of France
Adolf Hitler, chancellor of Germany
Ho Chi Minh, North Vietnamese leader
Alvin York, highly decorated American World War I soldier

SCIENCE
Ruth Benedict, American anthropologist
Richard E. Byrd, American explorer
Karl T. Compton, American physicist
Edwin Hubble, American astronomer
Paul W. Merrill, American astronomer
Hermann J. Muller, American scientist
Otto Stern, German physicist
Frits Zernike, Dutch physicist

LITERATURE

Agatha Christie, English writer

Jean Cocteau, French poet

T. S. Eliot, American poet

Marianne Moore, American poet

Boris Pasternak, Russian writer

John Reed, American writer and activist

Siegfried Sassoon, English poet

Edith Sitwell, English poet

RELIGION/PHILOSOPHY

Mary Baker Eddy, American Christian Scientist

Mohandas K. Gandhi, Indian political and spiritual leader, advocate of nonviolence

Martin Heidegger, German philosopher

Gabriel Marcel, French philosopher

Aimee Semple McPherson, Canadian evangelist

Francis Cardinal Spellman, American religious leader

Paul Tillich, German theologian

Ludwig Wittgenstein, Austrian philosopher

SPORTS

Grover Cleveland Alexander, American baseball player

Ty Cobb, American baseball player

Shoeless Joe Jackson, American baseball player

Walter Johnson, American baseball player

Knute Rockne, American football coach

Tris Speaker, American baseball player

Casey Stengel, American baseball player and manager

Jim Thorpe, American Olympic athlete

INDUSTRY/BUSINESS

Nikolai Bukharin, Russian economist

Conrad Hilton, American businessman and hotelier

Joseph P. Kennedy, American businessman and diplomat

Horace Liveright, American publisher

Alfieri Maserati, Italian businessman

Robert Moses, American New York City planner

Colonel Harlan Sanders, American businessman

Michio Suzuki, Japanese businessman

O'NEILL

in an
hour

OVERVIEW OF EUGENE O'NEILL'S ACHIEVEMENT

America's foremost playwright, Eugene Gladstone O'Neill, wrote in *The American Spectator* magazine in 1932, "One's outer life passes in a solitude haunted by the masks of others; one's inner life passes in a solitude hounded by the masks of oneself." Few dramatists have as succinctly described the central concern of their plays.

O'Neill emerged as a leading figure in American theater during World War I. Since then critics have taken pains to explain his significance and the complex themes and characters of his prolific output. Harold Bloom has written of the "inevitable oddity" that O'Neill has "no American precursors." This is despite two centuries of American theater and drama preceding him. Without question, O'Neill is a quintessentially American voice. Even so, there are many influences on his work — and many of them are acknowledged by O'Neill. They include modernist European dramatists from Henrik Ibsen to August Strindberg. O'Neill also looked to writers of classical tragedy, and a

---

diverse collection of philosophers and writers influenced him. These included Friedrich Nietzsche, Arthur Schopenhauer, and Sigmund Freud. However, Bloom considers that the "spiritual darkness" of O'Neill's plays comes not so much from these later influences, but from O'Neill's Irish-American Catholic heritage. Bloom also looks to the addictions and personal tragedies within O'Neill's immediate family that set him in a personal battle with his conception of God.

Eugene O'Neill was immensely successful during his lifetime, being awarded three Pulitzer Prizes for Drama during his life. Then he received a fourth after his death. He also became the only American dramatist to be honored with a Nobel Prize for Literature. Unfortunately, in all likelihood O'Neill felt he had failed to achieve his aesthetic goals as physical illness and deep depression stifled his work in the last decade of his life.

There is no doubt that O'Neill's commitment to rid the early twentieth-century American stage of the sentimental, melodramatic theater was as personal as it was intellectual. Melodramatic theater was the bread and butter of his father, celebrated nineteenth-century actor James O'Neill. His father made a fortune starring in the Alexandre Dumas melodrama *The Count of Monte Cristo*. O'Neill rejected and often mocked the stage practices of his father's day. Yet his earliest plays owe much to the melodramatic tradition. Without doubt, the rich and memorable characters populating O'Neill's plays are drawn from the richness of nineteenth-century stage tradition. Bold characterizations and acting were the norm.

The techniques of O'Neill's drama evolved well beyond those of his father's theater. At the same time, he threw down a gauntlet for all subsequent serious-minded American dramatists. The generation of American playwrights immediately preceding him included Bronson Howard, James A. Herne, William Vaughn Moody, Clyde Fitch, and Edward Sheldon. They seemed, in their individual ways, and in their finest works, to be reaching toward what O'Neill managed to achieve. Bloom refers to O'Neill's "ambiguous relation to our [America's] literary past." This results from his interest in the more advanced philosophies and literature of late nineteenth- and early twentieth-century Europe. It is also a result of his uneasy love-hate relationship with the American stage of his father's generation.

Despite the influence of late nineteenth- and early twentieth-century trends in philosophy on his work, O'Neill is an American playwright. Virtually all of his major writing was done between the two world wars. This time could fairly be described as an extraordinary era encompassing the tragedies of World War I, the Jazz Age, the Great Depression, and the gathering storm clouds of World War II.

These titanic events were set in a period of vast change. Rapid developments occurred in technology, economy, politics, and social mores. Of particular significance to O'Neill, the tastes of the theater-going audience were also changing. Prior to World War I, American drama tended toward the sentimental and melodramatic. Emphasis was on entertainment value. The theater had a long history of serving as a platform for sociopolitical debate and as a place for sharing communal history and concern. This was largely ignored by American playwrights until after World War I. By the end of the nineteenth century, a few serious-minded dramatists — James A. Herne, Clyde Fitch, William Vaughn Moody — attempted to establish the greater seriousness of purpose typical of the fin de siècle European theater. They drew on the plays of Henrik Ibsen, George Bernard Shaw, Anton Chekhov, and August Strindberg. However, audiences seemed largely disinterested. In fact, they were shocked by the content of these plays.

American attempts to stay out of World War I ultimately failed. President Woodrow Wilson, an intellectual with high ideals, reluctantly led the country into involvement in the catastrophic war. Wilson's more expansive worldview and the war itself took the country out of its long isolationism. This, coupled with the tragedies of the war, were catalysts for social changes that had been roiling American life since the mid-nineteenth century. The younger generation — O'Neill's generation — rejected much about pre-war American values.

This was particularly true in regard to economic justice, politics, race, religion, and sexuality. As the Jazz Age dawned, a new intellectualism, coupled with a desire for greater frankness in all matters, further sped progress in many areas. This was especially true regarding long-standing taboos. Women's skirts moved up several inches from the floor toward the knee. Young women bobbed their hair and smoked cigarettes. Finally, the decades-long struggle for suffrage prevailed. In the election of 1920, women voted for the first time. Changes were slower in other areas — particularly race relations. Discussion of such issues moved to the center of the national debate. Old values prevailed in some areas — temperance advocates managed to make prohibition the law of the land. Much of society responded by merely taking its drinking to "speakeasies." These were supposedly private nightclubs that were an open secret with local authorities. The law was flaunted in this area with serious results. Bootlegging of alcohol supplied criminals with access to riches beyond their wildest dreams. The resultant gang battles over turf led to unprecedented violence. Organized crime became a fact of American life.

When the decade-long post–World War I economic boom ended with the 1929 crash of the Wall Street stock market, the Great Depression began. This radically transformed the American landscape. With Franklin D. Roosevelt's election in 1932, the "New Deal" began. Again America faced new challenges from within and without its borders. The rise of fascism in Europe added new fears to the economic woes of the time. Fortunately, technological developments offered some hope for a brighter and better future. Improved transportation made the world a smaller place. Radio and sound films brought the news and entertainment to all. Meanwhile the Works Progress Administration (and other New Deal programs) employed many in the expansion and improvement of the nation's infrastructure.

Within less than twenty years, American society had undergone vast changes and tumultuous events that influenced a generation of writers and thinkers whose work flourished between the two world wars.

O'Neill's response to the American sociopolitical culture can be seen most vividly at the end of his career. In 1946, one of his last plays, *The Iceman Cometh*, opened to an unenthusiastic response on Broadway. In this play, O'Neill condemns a society in thrall to the wrong values. He stresses the false illusions and human weaknesses that he viewed as preventing the nation (not to mention the individual) from realizing its lofty and perhaps unreachable ideals. In responding to the post–World War II economic boom, O'Neill became a lone chronicler of an America on the wrong path. It was not unlike the times that followed World War I at the beginning of his career. He had long since rejected as hollow idols the freshly renewed values of materialism and conformity. As he stated in a 1946 interview quoted in Diggins, "I feel, in a sense, that America is the greatest failure in history. It was given everything, more than any other country in history, but we've squandered our soul by trying to possess something outside it, and we'll end as that game usually does, by losing our soul and that thing outside it too."

In many respects, O'Neill's value as a playwright rests not only on the startling ambition of his dramatic goals and his bold experiments in form, but on his solitary vision of a nation on the wrong path. Some of O'Neill's contemporaries — from the probing dramas of Robert E. Sherwood to the high comedies of Philip Barry — did not shy away from critical views of aspects of American values. But none looked into the darker corners of the American soul with the astringent analysis found in O'Neill's greatest plays.

O'Neill's politics were forged in the time of his intellectual awakening in the Greenwich Village of 1910. As a seething young radical and aspiring playwright, O'Neill became aware of a deep chasm between American optimism and the harsher truths of a society in the grip of materialism. He also saw deep racial and ethnic prejudices as well as anti-intellectualism. These he feared shattered any true hope of genuine democracy. O'Neill's plays gain their undeniable power from a split between deep longings for a utopian future and the individual's eternal struggle for freedom and spiritual fulfillment. Thus the tragedy faced by O'Neill's central characters stems from an ultimate recognition of the crushing loss inherent in this split. Regardless of the setting of any O'Neill play, or the distinctly individual desires of any of his characters, this disillusionment changes and often destroys them.

Finally, O'Neill's continued worth as a dramatist extends beyond the emotional power and scope of his tragic dramas. It extends to his role as a harbinger of a deeply anxious culture adrift in the deceptions of deluded and corrupt leaders and false values largely unchallenged by a hapless population drugged by empty amusements and divisiveness. For O'Neill, the search for true liberty and truth in his solitary dramatic journey remains unrealized.

EUGENE O'NEILL'S EARLY LIFE

As the son of one of the nineteenth century's most celebrated actors, O'Neill surely had the American theater in his blood from birth. He was born on October 16, 1888, at the Barrett Hotel in what at the time was slowly becoming New York City's theater district. His father, James O'Neill, had already achieved notable success in a range of roles, including Shakespeare and dramas with a religious theme. Then he scored an enormous personal success in *The Count of Monte Cristo*, which he played for the first time in 1883. O'Neill's mother, Mary Ellen "Ella" Quinlan, had married his father in 1877 over the objections of her family. She gave birth to O'Neill's two brothers, James "Jamie" O'Neill and Edmund Burke O'Neill.

The death of Edmund from measles in 1885, three years before O'Neill's birth, is considered a seminal event. It ignited decades of family tragedy for the O'Neills. Ella fought a solitary battle with morphine addiction, which was later made worse by the difficult birth of Eugene. Both Jamie and Eugene became alcoholics, not to mention their father's overindulgence in drink. Many details of the O'Neill family difficulties are changed or made wholly fictional in O'Neill's masterwork, *Long Day's Journey Into Night*. The play also included ideas drawn from the experiences of O'Neill's third wife, Carlotta Monterey. Yet the play can be regarded as capturing the essence of each family member through the merging of fact and fiction. Jamie's ultimate death resulting from alcoholism and despair over his mother's death in 1922 is examined in O'Neill's final play, *A Moon for the Misbegotten*. In this play, the character of James Tyrone Jr., Jamie's alter ego, is continued from *Long Day's Journey Into Night*.

In 1884, James O'Neill Sr. purchased a house in New London, Connecticut, while visiting Ella's mother there. For the next thirty-five years, the O'Neills spent most summers at the house they named the "Monte Cristo Cottage." It was located on Pequot Avenue, overlooking Connecticut's Thames River. It also provided the setting for *Long Day's Journey Into Night*. A more fictionalized (and romanticized) treatment of New London environs can be found in O'Neill's *Ah, Wilderness!* During the rest of the year, O'Neill Sr., usually with Ella and their sons in tow, barnstormed the United States with *The Count of Monte Cristo*. The play became both his fortune and his albatross, as audiences seemed more and more reluctant to see him in any other role.

Family life improved for the O'Neills with Ella's final defeat of her morphine addiction in 1914 (although some biographers believe she suffered a relapse in 1917 when she endured a mastectomy). Jamie's descent into alcoholism caused distress. Unfortunately, Eugene O'Neill's various rebellions against his father caused more tensions. Then he found a new sense of purpose following months in a sanitarium to cure tuberculosis in 1912. The haunted passions of O'Neill's plays reflect a profoundly damaged man. The inevitable autobiographical elements in his work merged with his views on a societal psychosis. This he believed was fueled by deep (and often unspoken) conflicts and contradictions springing from a national obsession with materialism, technology, and a futile search for spiritual transcendence. At the same time, the plays reflect a complex tangle of psychological, moral, political, and spiritual dilemmas submerged within the American consciousness. These paralleled his early family life.

Long Day's Journey Into Night is the most overtly autobiographical of O'Neill's plays. It obviously demonstrates the family dysfunction in which he was trapped with his father, mother, and brother. Even long after their deaths in the early 1920s, O'Neill's writing returned to them. In fact, it could be said that after the failure of *Days Without End* in 1934, O'Neill returned entirely to the concerns of his early life. He returned not only to his family but also to the watershed year of 1912. At this point, on the brink of suicide, O'Neill broke free of the hold of his family. He found an intellectual and political mission for himself. Then he gave himself over, with a breathtaking completeness (even to the point of casting aside wives and children) to the unreachable goals of his dramatic ambition.

The autobiographical elements of O'Neill's plays and their intellectual foundation are grounded in his agonized autobiography. The guilt and pain of loss, betrayal, and love, and the despair of longing for a spiritual transcendence he felt was somehow denied him were all part of what he drew on. His nature was profoundly divided. He was drawn to his family on a near-primal level, yet repelled from its failure to sustain him. In this period, O'Neill chose to identify himself (and to implant his central characters) with an abiding concern with profoundly American issues of race, ethnicity, class, and faith. These were often seen through the lens of his warped views of family life and the isolated struggle of the individual.

In this seminal period, in which his son's drama was formed in the crucible of family tragedy and radical politics, James O'Neill's career was nearing its end. He was praised by contemporary critics for an acting style more natural than most of his peers. But his brand of romantic theater was rapidly superseded by a more realistic and serious drama. His son became the driving force in the late 1910s of this new style. The senior O'Neill expressed reservations about the modernist themes of his son's early dramas, feeling the theater's central purpose was escapism. He found Eugene's one-act plays of 1910 depressing. Yet despite his final illness, James O'Neill was in proud attendance at the

1920 Broadway opening of his son's play *Beyond the Horizon*. O'Neill won the first of four Pulitzer Prizes for Drama for this play.

Following a stroke that year, James O'Neill entered a New London hospital, where he died on August 10, 1920. Ella faced a recurrence of her cancer in 1919 while attempting to assist Jamie, whose alcoholism had spun out of control. With her help, he quit drinking and lived with Ella in Los Angeles, California, until she suffered a stroke and died on February 28, 1922. Jamie escorted Ella's body east by train, falling into a completely alcoholic state. He was so lost in drink that he was unable to attend her funeral service at St. Leo's Church in New York City, followed by burial in New London, Connecticut. After Ella's death, Jamie returned to his old ways and drank himself to death a year later. His experiences following his mother's death were sadly dramatized in Eugene's final play, *A Moon for the Misbegotten*. This play, like O'Neill's greatest plays, drew its power from his personal life.

Long Day's Journey Into Night and *A Moon for the Misbegotten*, drawn so directly from O'Neill's personal life, oddly came at the end of his playwriting career and years after the events. Perhaps the distance of time allowed the clarity he needed to dramatize his parents and brother. O'Neill's work may be helpfully divided into three eras. The first period (1912 to 1920) found him searching for his voice and style. The second era (1920 to 1935) was an intensely productive and experimental phase. He concluded with the most personal and least overtly experimental of his works, written roughly between 1935 and 1943.

By 1920, O'Neill was established as a leading figure in American theater. He found success in his personal life more elusive. Troubled relations with his father led a youthful O'Neill to escape into an ill-conceived marriage producing one son, Eugene O'Neill Jr. This brief union ended almost immediately. It was followed by a second marriage to writer Agnes Boulton. This resulted in the births of a son, Shane, and a daughter, Oona. This marriage also ended in divorce after O'Neill began an affair with actress Carlotta Monterey. They married in 1929.

By the mid-1930s, O'Neill began to suffer various health problems, including a tremor in his hands that was believed to be Parkinson's disease. It was not, although its effects were no less devastating. The tremor hampered his ability to work, although he continued to write until 1943. He largely withdrew from active participation in the production of his plays. His last years were difficult, due in part to a frequently troubled relationship with his wife, estrangement from his children, and the decline of his theatrical fortunes. These included the relative failures of the last two new O'Neill plays produced during his life, *The Iceman Cometh* in 1946 and *A Moon for the Misbegotten* in 1947.

O'Neill may well have died believing himself a forgotten figure of the American theater's rise after World War I. Fortunately, within three years of his death in 1953, an O'Neill renaissance would begin with the Broadway production of *Long Day's Journey Into Night*. This has continued unabated into the twenty-first century.

WORK: STAGE ONE (1912–1920)

O'Neill won a reputation as the first internationally significant U.S. playwright. He wrote more than sixty one-act and full-length plays, receiving four Pulitzer Prizes and the Nobel Prize for Literature in 1936. As previously indicated, he spent most of his early childhood barnstorming the United States with his parents and elder brother Jamie. Then he enrolled in Catholic boarding schools, and ultimately, for a troubled year at Princeton University. Poor academic performance at Princeton led to his dismissal. After leaving Princeton, he worked at odd jobs (including with his father's theatrical troupe) and as a seaman, traveling to South America and Europe. In 1912, following his return from sea, O'Neill fell into an alcoholic period, living in or near wharf-side saloons and frequenting brothels. At an extremely low ebb in his fortunes and health, O'Neill attempted suicide. Then, after being diagnosed with tuberculosis, he spent much of 1912 in a sanitarium. To fill his time, O'Neill read the classics and masterworks of modern literature, drama, and philosophy. This led him to a decision to pursue a playwriting career. He sought guidance from Harvard University drama professor George Pierce Baker. He then enrolled as a special student in Baker's English 47 class, a unique playwriting workshop. Under Baker's guidance, O'Neill wrote a few plays, now lost. After leaving the workshop, O'Neill continued to write on his own. He published a collection of his earliest plays with support from his father, who bankrolled the printing of the book.

It was not until O'Neill spent the summer of 1916 in Provincetown, Massachusetts, on Cape Cod, that he came into his own as a dramatist. A small group of radical young artists and writers had formed a little theater they called the Provincetown Players. They used an abandoned wharf-side building as their theater. They were led by George Cram "Jig" Cook and his wife, aspiring playwright Susan Glaspell. The group also included John Reed and Louise Bryant, with whom O'Neill began an affair. Others involved at various points included Neith Boyce, Michael Gold, and Robert Edmond Jones. They were joined by Mabel Dodge, Edna St. Vincent Millay, Cleon Throckmorton, and William and Marguerite Zorach. If O'Neill discovered his power as a dramatist with the Players, they discovered their mission — promoting O'Neill's plays. They produced O'Neill's one-acts, beginning with *Bound East for Cardiff* and *Thirst*.

A small amateur operation, the members of the Players handled many tasks, and O'Neill himself acted in both plays. During this time, he wrote other one-acts. These included *Before Breakfast* and *The G.A.N.* (the latter of which is destroyed). He also wrote a full-length play, *Now I Ask You*, and a short story, *Tomorrow*.

In the fall, the Provincetown Players moved their operations from Cape Cod to New York City. There they successfully performed O'Neill's *Bound East for Cardiff* and *Before Breakfast*. After two seasons in a space at 139 MacDougal Street, the Players made their permanent home in a former stable at 133 MacDougal Street. Here they produced nearly one hundred plays in eight seasons. These were written by forty-seven different American authors. The Players shut down in 1922 at the peak of their success, when O'Neill's Expressionist play *The Hairy Ape* was transferred to a Broadway theater.

As previously noted, O'Neill's dramatic output can be usefully divided into three distinct eras. From 1912 to 1920 he typically wrote one-act plays depicting the lives of seafaring men and the denizens of dockside saloons. From 1920 to 1935 he wrote full-length experimental dramas. These often featured influences such as the techniques of classical tragedy and often included Expressionistic elements, masks, spoken asides, and other meta-theatrical devices. These plays were aimed at revealing O'Neill's themes centering on existence as a battle of man versus fate (or God). Then, from 1935 to 1943, he wrote psychologically complex, naturalistically stark, personal dramas. These were drawn directly (if somewhat fictitiously) from his own life experiences.

At the height of the second phase, O'Neill also planned a seven-to-eleven-play cycle, *A Tale of Possessors Self-Dispossessed*. Of these he completed only *A Touch of the Poet* (1939) and a lengthy draft of *More Stately Mansions* (1939). This generation-by-generation chronicle was of an Irish-American family tragically entrapped by their possessions and a legacy of family betrayals. This was to be complemented by a projected cycle of one-act character studies with the overarching title *By Way of Obit*. But this was also aborted, with the exception of one completed play, *Hughie* (1942).

O'Neill's themes began to take shape, however, from the first phase of his work. He created classically inspired heroes. These were conceived from a merging of his conflicted feelings about his Irish-Catholic upbringing with the psychological theories of Sigmund Freud and Carl Jung. He drew as well from the philosophical writings of Friedrich Nietzsche. He also looked to the plays of Henrik Ibsen, August Strindberg, Gerhardt Hauptmann, and other European modernists. It was not until his second phase as a playwright that O'Neill's experimental, thematically challenging works dominated Broadway.

But despite the acclaim achieved by many of these works, his most performed and critically acclaimed works are those from the final phase of his career. These include *The Iceman Cometh*, *Long Day's Journey Into Night*, and *A Moon for the Misbegotten*. The surviving works from the two unfinished cycles are also seminal.

There is little doubt that O'Neill began playwriting in his first period with the goal of expunging the sentimental, melodramatic (and often shallow) trappings of the commercialized popular theater. He intended to replace it with a serious, ambitious American drama. This he built on modernist thought and cutting-edge European theatrical experimentation. However, O'Neill's plays, particularly those of his first two periods, are as much a product of the nineteenth-century popular stage as they are a rejection of it. Occasionally sentimental and owing much to the epic scale of melodrama, O'Neill nevertheless aimed for, and often achieved, a loftier tragic vision. He was able to do this even in his earliest works. In his finest plays, O'Neill, like Ibsen and Strindberg, captures moments of deep psychological anguish. He also explores the isolation and moral confusion of modern life. To do this he used his own reconception of Henrik Ibsen's "saving lies." These are the illusions necessary to survive the vicissitudes of existence. More importantly, O'Neill's plays are profoundly influenced by his personal spiritual struggle and the dysfunction of his family.

O'Neill's early one-acts included *Bound East for Cardiff* (1916), *The Long Voyage Home* (1917), *In the Zone* (1917), *Ile* (1917), and *The Moon of the Caribbees* (1918), among others. These plays established his reputation and led to ambitious full-length dramas. The first was *Beyond the Horizon*. O'Neill wrote it in 1918. It was produced on Broadway in 1920. It received positive critical response and a Pulitzer Prize for Drama. This established O'Neill as a force. Even O'Neill's father, an exemplar of the melodramatic stage O'Neill sought to banish, was powerfully impressed with *Beyond the Horizon*.

Beyond the Horizon is, in many respects, a culmination of themes O'Neill had previously explored in his one-act plays of the 1910s. The play's central character, Rob Mayo, is a dreamy aspiring poet longing to escape rural New England in order to see the world. His brother, Andrew, relishes the idea of managing the family farm and marrying Ruth, who lives on the neighboring farm. Fate intervenes when Ruth reveals her passion for Rob. This results in the brothers trading destinies, with ultimately tragic results. *Beyond the Horizon* opened on February 3, 1920, at the Morosco Theatre for 111 performances. Some critics recognized that this three-act play was the true beginning of a serious modern American drama. O'Neill used the novel device of jumping ahead five years during each intermission. The critical response to *Beyond the Horizon*, and the Pulitzer Prize, firmly established O'Neill's reputation. He embarked on fifteen years of extraordinary experimentation and productivity.

WORK: STAGE TWO (1920–1935)

The critical praise that met *Beyond the Horizon* would be repeated numerous times between 1920 and 1935. O'Neill did experience occasional failures as he stretched the bounds of his own talent and challenged audiences more accustomed to sentimental and melodramatic fare. He also grappled with his alcoholic tendencies, increasing health problems, and family troubles. O'Neill framed themes taken from his own troubled family dynamics throughout his career. In *Beyond the Horizon* he explored sibling rivalry and lost dreams. He also looked at shattered faith, and the multiple disillusionments of contemporary life (including modern faith in technology and progress). O'Neill's major works during the first of this period included *The Emperor Jones* (1920), *"Anna Christie"* (1920), and *The Hairy Ape* (1921). Next he wrote *All God's Chillun Got Wings* (1923) and *Desire Under the Elms* (1924). Then in 1925, he wrote *The Great God Brown*. He followed this with *Marco Millions* (1925), *Lazarus Laughed* (1927), and *Strange Interlude* (1927). In 1929, he wrote *Dynamo*. He produced *Mourning Becomes Electra* in 1931. In 1932 he wrote his only comedy,

Ah, Wilderness! (1932). These plays exhibit characteristics of American lyric realism as well as bolder, more theatrical experiments.

O'Neill's prolific output — and the production of his work on Broadway — declined after the failure of *Days Without End* in 1934. O'Neill mostly withdrew from active production of his plays. Despite receiving the Nobel Prize for Literature in 1936, he did not agree to a Broadway production of any new work. More than a decade later he allowed *The Iceman Cometh* (1946) to be produced.

In the three major stages of O'Neill's work, the thematic terrain of his dramas is suffused with a starkly tragic sensibility. This is often mixed with a romanticizing strain (even as O'Neill often mocks such attitudes). He focuses on the depths of the human psyche. He also draws on the nihilistic views of Nietzsche and the psychological theories of Freud and Jung.

The range and diversity of his dramatic experimentation and thematic concerns is manifested in many ways. For example, in his only comedy, *Ah, Wilderness!*, O'Neill abandons the grim tragic view typical of his work. Here he affectionately portrays a loving father guiding a teenage son through a bittersweet coming-of-age. The play is set in turn-of-the-century Connecticut. It has a slightly darker subplot involving the failed relationship of an alcoholic uncle and maiden aunt. But generally, in *Ah, Wilderness!* O'Neill demonstrates a lightness of touch that is seen nowhere in the rest of his work. Critics were stunned by this demonstration of versatility.

More typically, in *Long Day's Journey Into Night*, O'Neill reveals familial relations as profoundly flawed in a semi-autobiographical drama. The father, mother, and two adult sons are inextricably bound together by their love, failings, addictions, and guilts. They share a profound sense of loss epitomized in the failure of the mother to defeat an addiction to morphine. In *Mourning Becomes Electra*, O'Neill writes a towering trilogy freely adapted from Aeschylus' *Oresteia*. The sins of the father and mother are visited on their adult children in classical style. O'Neill sets the play in the aftermath of the American Civil

War. Then he folds in the modernist concerns typical of his 1920s–30s work. Further, in *Desire Under the Elms*, in which O'Neill was partially inspired by Sophocles' *Oedipus Rex*, he depicts a son's illicit relations with his father's young wife.

In pursuit of a modern spiritual belief independent of established religions and value systems, O'Neill's central characters often find themselves isolated from their society as they attempt to forge a new myth for belief. Sometimes, faith is found (and lost) in modern technology, as in *Dynamo*. For O'Neill, the great machines of industry are dehumanizing He explored this idea earlier in the Expressionistic *The Hairy Ape*. Daringly for his time, O'Neill also dealt with America's racial attitudes in *All God's Chillun Got Wings*. In this play, he depicts a tragic relationship (and marriage) between a black man and a white woman. In his plays, O'Neill's characters, whatever their individual problems or qualities, believe themselves to be godforsaken, lost souls. They long for salvation and more satisfying human connections, even as they themselves are inadequate to the task of forging such bonds. They are profoundly alone in their struggles. Down-and-out Broadway gambler Erie Smith of *Hughie* cries out in grief for his dead pal, "Christ, it's lonely." His existential anguish reveals the longing for salvation among the bruised souls of O'Neill's plays.

Following the success of *Beyond the Horizon*, O'Neill again challenged his audience with *The Emperor Jones*. It opened first in a Provincetown Players production on November 1, 1920, and moved to Broadway's Selwyn Theatre on December 27, 1920. Borrowing on the techniques of German theatrical and cinematic Expressionism, this eight-scene tragedy was directed by George Cram "Jig" Cook and designed by Cleon Throckmorton. The play broke through a racial barrier with actor Charles Gilpin in the title role. It was the first major role played by an African American in a drama on Broadway. Although the role would become closely associated with Paul Robeson, who took over for Gilpin and also played it in the 1933 screen adaptation, Gilpin was praised for his strong performance as Brutus Jones. Jones was a former Pullman porter who, prior to the play's beginning, arrived as a stowaway at an island in the West Indies. Once there, he sets himself up as emperor of a native tribe. Emulating the greed he observed in white businessmen traveling on trains, Jones steals from his subjects. He plans to escape with his riches before a revolt can be organized, as he brags to Smithers, a white Cockney trader. Smithers warns Jones that an ominous drumbeat heard in the distance signals preparations for an uprising, but Jones is unconcerned since he has convinced his subjects that he can only be killed by a silver bullet. Jones's confidence dissolves, however, as he gets lost in the jungle and in the labyrinth of his own mind. Increasingly phantasmagoric visions show him his own past and his subconscious racial memory. These include a vision of a witch doctor persuading Jones to offer himself as a sacrifice. The incessant distant drumbeats reflect Jones's mounting terror. The drumbeats cease only when a silver bullet — cast from melted coins by the rebelling natives — ends his life. The play was renowned for its Expressionist experiment with sound. A tom-tom begins thumping at normal pulse rate — 72 beats per minute — and steadily accelerates during Jones's increasingly hallucinogenic flight through the jungle by night.

Remarkably, on the same day *The Emperor Jones* shifted to Broadway, O'Neill's *Diff'rent* opened in a Provincetown Players production. It ultimately moved to Broadway as well. One of the least produced of O'Neill's full-length plays, *Diff'rent* focused on a romance stunted by puritanical attitudes. Actress Mary Blair is a young woman who becomes a foolish spinster not unlike those Tennessee Williams crafted two decades later in his most emblematic plays.

During 1921, more critical attention was paid to O'Neill's *"Anna Christie,"* a moody, character-driven drama. Revised from an earlier O'Neill play, *Chris Christopherson*, it was directed by Arthur Hopkins, designed by Robert Edmond Jones, and featured Pauline Lord in the title role. Opening on November 2, 1921, at the Vanderbilt Theatre, *"Anna Christie"* ran for 177 performances. It subsequently became one of O'Neill's most frequently produced works. In 1930, it became a famous screen adaptation starring Greta Garbo in her first "talkie" role as a hard-drinking prostitute. She delivers her first line, "Gimme a whiskey — ginger ale on the side. And don't be stingy baby," when entering Johnny-the-Priest's wharf-side saloon. The location was based on the actual New York dockside barroom O'Neill frequented a decade earlier.

"Anna Christie" is fraught with the familial tensions typical of many O'Neill plays. Scandinavian seaman Chris Christopherson awaits Anna, the grown daughter he has not seen since she was a child. Believing that Anna would be better off living on a farm in Minnesota, Chris had sent her there. He does not know she suffered sexual abuse at the hands of a cousin during her adolescence or that to support herself she works as a prostitute on the streets of St. Paul. When Anna arrives, exhausted, despairing, and alcoholic, she is rejuvenated by her proximity to the sea. She describes it as something lost that she had been longing to find again. The sea is a healing environment in many O'Neill works.

Anna manages to keep her profession a secret for a time. Gradually, her father's shipmate, Mat Burke, falls in love with her and proposes marriage. Anna, feeling unworthy, confesses her sordid past. As a result, both Mat and Chris go on a bender and sign up for long hitches at sea. Before departing, however, they reconcile with Anna, who promises to await their return.

Actresses as diverse as Celeste Holm, Liv Ullman, and Natasha Richardson have played Anna in notable revivals of the play. Among the leading women characters of his plays, Anna, Nina Leeds in *Strange Interlude*, and Mary Tyrone in *Long Day's Journey Into Night* demonstrate that O'Neill could write women characters as effectively as the male protagonists who more typically dominate his plays

"Anna Christie" is among O'Neill's more realistic dramas. He continued his experimentation with Expressionist techniques with *The Hairy Ape*. It opened on March 9, 1922, at the Provincetown Theatre and ran for 120 performances. Its Expressionistic design elements by Robert Edmond Jones and Cleon Throckmorton created a nightmarish quality admired by critics of the original production. The nightmare belongs to "Yank" Smith, a grimy, inarticulate stoker on a steamship. He was played in the original production by Louis Wolheim. When a wealthy young socialite, Mildred Douglas, is allowed to visit the boiler room, she faints upon seeing Yank. This disturbing vision of another mode of existence sparks Yank's soul-searching journey when the ship docks in New York. He visits Mildred's world, Fifth Avenue. His rage at the high life of the "swells" results in his arrest. Even in jail, Yank doesn't fit in. Upon release he attends a meeting of the IWW, the leftist International Workers of the World, or "Wobblies." He offers to blow up the Douglas Steel Works for them, but they reject him. Seeking to belong somewhere, Yank visits the gorilla cage at the zoo. He attempts to set the beast free, but it crushes him in its powerful embrace. The play is subtitled "A Comedy of Ancient and Modern Life." It stresses the alienation of the individual in a technological, capitalist society. Like *Anna Christie,* it is among O'Neill's most-revived works. In 1944, a botched screen version featured William Bendix and Susan Hayward.

The themes of *The Hairy Ape,* centering on an individual who does not fit into the world, were explored in greater depth, and with considerable attendant controversy, when O'Neill's *All God's Chillun Got Wings* opened at the Provincetown Playhouse. It opened on May 15, 1924, for a disappointing forty-three performances. James Light directed this two-act drama that explored the explosive topic of mixing races. The play caused a major furor in its first production. O'Neill received death threats from the Ku Klux Klan and others. New York City's license commissioner pondered closing the production on reports that white actress Mary Blair, in the role of Ella Downey, would kiss the hand of African-American actor Paul Robeson. The Gerry Society also raised concerns over the employment of child actors in what it considered a scandalous production.

However, it was clear that the central controversy stemmed from the depiction of a lifelong and genuine relationship between Jim and

Ella. They love each other, but Ella is aware that prevailing racial attitudes preclude a marital relationship. She becomes involved with a
white man and has a child by him. When she is deserted and the child
dies, the defeated Ella turns back to Jim. They marry, but she is
haunted by their racial difference. She is so fearful of societal reaction
that her precarious grip on sanity slips away. Reduced to a childlike
state, Ella is cared for by the eternally loving Jim.

All God's Chillun Got Wings, a sadly bitter play on the human toll of
prejudice, only barely preceded another controversial O'Neill play, *Desire Under the Elms*, which opened on November 11, 1924, at the
Greenwich Village Theatre. This time, however, the controversy sur-
rounding this play attracted audiences, resulting in a 208-performance
run. This three-part drama was inspired by O'Neill's love of classical
tragedy — in this case, the Hippolytus/Phaedra myth. The play focused
on father and son tensions in a frank depiction of sexuality, incest, and
violence well beyond the accepted standards of its time. New York authorities, including the district attorney, attempted to close the play
when moral crusaders objected to its steamy subject matter. In England,
Desire Under the Elms was also banned until 1940. It was banned in
some American cities, despite general acclaim by critics and audiences.

Robert Edmond Jones designed *Desire Under the Elms* impression-
istically. He also directed its first production. The play is set in 1850
on a stark New England farm. Ephraim Cabot, a flinty and cold
seventy-five-year-old Puritan, owns the property. He has turned the
rugged, stony terrain into a handsome farm. The land is bound together with his stern theology, which he expresses in hubristic pride at
defeating nature's harsh demands. O'Neill begins the play as Ephraim's
two elder sons sell their stakes in the farm to their younger half-
brother, Eben. They then leave for California to escape their father's
harshness. Eben's mother, who actually owned the farm, has recently
died. Ephraim decides to marry a much younger widow, Abbie Putnam, essentially dispossessing Eben, who will have to see his mother's
farm pass to this new wife. O'Neill thusly establishes a central conflict

between father and son, whose relationship is already tense. Abbie resists Ephraim. When he tells her she will inherit the farm if she gives him a son, Abbie's deep-seated ambitions are ignited. She longs for security, but she does not comprehend that her presence is making the conflicts between Ephraim and Eben worse. Ephraim impatiently awaits the possibility of a new son he imagines as his route to immortality. But, as O'Neill makes clear, the child represents a means of rejecting Eben. Ephraim, in his egocentric, single-minded devotion to the farm, confuses himself with the land. He believes that his unyielding work ethic results from a solitary battle he has waged against God and nature.

Eben feels unloved and dispossessed by his father. He desires to possess those things the old man loves most: the farm and Ephraim's new wife. Abbie, a sensuous woman, is the embodiment of both desires, and Eben is strongly attracted to her. His attraction is not only sexual but also a result of his deep maternal longings. Abbie is also drawn to Eben. When Ephraim's demands become too oppressive, she turns to Eben for comfort, stealing into his room in the night. They express their dreams and desires to each other, and their relationship is sexually consummated. This expression of their desires is enhanced by its illicit nature, for both must keep it a secret from Ephraim. Eben and Abbie live for stolen private moments together, but their secret is jeopardized when Abbie becomes pregnant with Eben's child. Ephraim does not question the pregnancy — he is too overjoyed about a new possession. This further inflames conflicts with Eben. When Ephraim throws a party celebrating the child's birth, the truth about its parentage comes out. Infuriated, the humiliated Ephraim convinces Eben that Abbie does not love him and only cares for the child as a means of inheriting the farm. Confused, Eben rejects Abbie, who is devastated. In a horrific act typical of the Greek tragedies that inspired O'Neill in creating *Desire Under the Elms*, Abbie kills the child in a twisted desire to prove her love for Eben. Only in the wake of this tragedy does Eben realize his own true feelings for Abbie. In an act of atonement, he insists on sharing responsibility for the child's murder. When authorities arrive to arrest them, they are led away hand in hand. Ephraim, having destroyed his family through his unforgiving rigidity, is left behind with only the rocky landscape for comfort.

In this quintessential O'Neill play, he makes use of New England dialects for the characters. He also imbues the play with Biblical elements (Ephraim, for example, seems a character out of the Old Testament). This approach helps elevate the play's language and idiom above the realistic style of much early-twentieth-century drama. Clearly, O'Neill was striving for a poetic language only slightly beyond realistic speech. He was also looking for a way for the characters to more directly express themselves beyond the dialectics of realism. In most of his Stage Two plays, O'Neill experimented with these concerns, using masks, spoken asides, Expressionistic techniques, and other devices to break free of realistic constraints. However, *Desire Under the Elms*, which contains a few central symbols, is also a highly naturalistic drama. This quality emerges, in part, from the sexually explicit actions of its characters and the detailed depiction of the harsh realities of nineteenth-century farm life. Despite its controversial elements, critics expressed admiration for *Desire Under the Elms*. They also praised the performances of the actors and overall production. Walter Huston won particular acclaim as Ephraim, from the critics and from O'Neill himself. O'Neill's unsparing study of family strife, greed, and untamed sexuality has steadily gained recognition as one of his finest accomplishments of the 1920s.

Following *Desire Under the Elms*, O'Neill's early seafaring plays were presented by the Provincetown Players. They titled the series *S. S. Glencairn* (the name of the ship featured in the plays). Four of the most realistic of O'Neill's one-acts, *The Moon of the Caribbees* (1918), *Bound East for Cardiff* (1916), *The Long Voyage Home* (1917), and *In the Zone* (1917), made up the bill. It opened on November 3, 1925, at New York's Provincetown Playhouse for 105 performances. The bill was revived for ninety additional performances on January 9, 1929. Film director John Ford later adapted these plays to the screen as *The Long Voyage Home* (1940), starring John Wayne. O'Neill felt this was the best screen adaptation of his work.

Moving on with new work, O'Neill continued his experimentation. This time, in *The Great God Brown*, he made central use of theatrical masks. It opened at the Greenwich Village Theatre on January 23, 1926, for 271 performances. The play won general praise from critics, despite bafflement on the part of some critics and audiences over O'Neill's use of masks, which he used to display the dual natures of his characters.

The Great God Brown examines two young men, William A. Brown and Dion Anthony, the sons of business partners. Each wears masks displaying appealing personas. A young woman, Margaret, attracts the attention of both men, but she is most drawn to Dion's gentle, sensitive mask. He has rejected business to be an artist. But when they find themselves in a moment of passion, Dion removes his mask ,revealing a darker persona beneath. Margaret recoils and Dion dies in grief. She marries William after he takes up Dion's sensitive mask. But he too dies as a result of denying his true persona, finding his only comfort with Cybel, a prostitute. Years after the death of both men, Margaret remains true to Dion's idealistic mask. O'Neill considered *The Great God Brown* his finest work. It has had few revivals, perhaps since the use of masks is too overt a device for an otherwise realistic drama.

The Great God Brown was driven, in part, by Dion's rejection of business for a life in art. O'Neill indicts the excesses of materialism in his next important work, *Marco Millions*. On the surface, *Marco Millions* in its original production was an opulent historical drama about Marco Polo. However, its concerns, particularly those about capitalism, were decidedly contemporary. It opened on January 9, 1928, in a Theatre Guild production. Rouben Mamoulian directed, with scene designs by Lee Simonson. Alfred Lunt played the title role. O'Neill's conception of Marco Polo's idealism corrupted by crassly materialistic desires was expressed through the death of the Princess of Cathay. She dies heartbroken over his betrayal of his more noble characteristics. The play's emphasis on the hollowness of wealth was prescient. Unfortunately, it did not resonate with audiences in the heady boom times of 1928. It ran for only 102 performances, a major disappointment for O'Neill. A revival, in 1930, after the crash of the stock market, failed even more resoundingly, running for a mere eight performances.

Another disappointment came with O'Neill's *Lazarus Laughed*. This was his only play of the era that was not produced on Broadway. Instead, it gave its only performances at California's Pasadena Playhouse, where it opened for a limited run on April 9, 1928. In this epic, biblically inspired work, O'Neill continued his experimentation with masks. In this case, he put the entire cast in masks with the exception of Lazarus. Lazarus's lack of a mask demonstrated that he did not fear death.

In *Lazarus Laughed*, Pompeia, a wildly jealous woman, kills Lazarus's wife in a fit of passion. Lazarus forgives her. The insane Caligula, who cannot understand this, condemns Lazarus to be burned at the stake. The repentant Pompeia throws herself on the fire, and Lazarus can only laugh as flames engulf him. He calls out "Fear not, Caligula! There is no death," as the horrified Caligula begs forgiveness. California critics applauded the lavish production, featuring Irving Pichel as Lazarus and Victor Jory as Caligula. Unfortunately, they were muted in their response to the play

Similar apathy met another O'Neill drama in this era, *Dynamo*. O'Neill planned it as the first of three plays about the ways in which science and modern technology were emerging as a new American religion. He also continued his experimentation with Expressionistic techniques. Plans for completion of the trilogy were abandoned, however, when *Dynamo* failed to impress critics and audiences. It opened on February 11, 1929, at the Martin Beck Theatre for a mere fifty performances.

Dynamo centers on Ada Fife, an atheist's daughter, who falls in love with Reuben Light, a minister's son. Reverend Light disapproves of Reuben's relationship with Ada, the daughter of his sworn enemy.

Angrily, Reuben denounces the faith of his family and leaves home. Attracted to the technological wonders of the day, Reuben makes science his only faith. When Ada seduces him in a hydroelectric plant, he kills her in a fit of guilt. Then he plunges into the dynamo, killing himself.

In her first important role, Claudette Colbert played Ada opposite Glenn Anders. They were directed by Philip Moeller. Lee Simonson garnered most of the critical plaudits for his impressive setting at the hydroelectric plant. Unfortunately, critics felt the significance of the play's subject was obscured by its grim plot.

Dynamo's failure was somewhat mitigated by the enormous success a year earlier of O'Neill's *Strange Interlude*, which was still running when *Dynamo* failed. *Strange Interlude* brought O'Neill an unprecedented third Pulitzer Prize for Drama following its opening on January 30, 1928. It ran at the Golden Theatre for 426 performances. It was produced by the Theatre Guild, Philip Moeller directing, with settings by Jo Mielziner. O'Neill made many innovations in this play, such as his use of asides. These allowed characters' private thoughts to be spoken aloud for the audience to hear. The play daringly focused on sexual psychology as a motivating factor, and it openly discussed an abortion. *Strange Interlude* was extraordinarily long, lasting for nine acts. Its action spread across twenty-five years (1919–1944) in the lives of the characters. Starting at 5:15 PM, performances of *Strange Interlude* included a dinner break.

The central figure of *Strange Interlude*, Nina Leeds, was played by Lynn Fontanne in the original production. Nina is resentful of her father's having prevented her marriage to her fiancé, Gordon, a pilot, before the war. With Gordon dead in the war, she devotes herself to nursing soldiers. A year later, Nina's father has died, and she has become openly promiscuous. The three significant men in her life are deeply concerned. They are the avuncular Charles Marsden, the willowy Sam Evans, and the rational-minded Edmund Darrell. They are all drawn to Nina, though they sense the presence of Gordon's ghost. Nina marries Sam. Before she tells him of his impending fatherhood, Sam's mother informs Nina that Sam carries a hereditary form of insanity. She convinces Nina to get an abortion, even suggesting that Nina give Sam a child by another man. Eventually Nina propositions Darrell. By the time she is with child by Darrell, Nina has transferred her ardor to him. She still carries on the charade of marriage with her husband, Sam.

Nina dominates the men she sees as father-substitutes (Marsden), husbands (Sam), and lovers (Darrell); her infant son Gordon is a fourth. When the play's action jumps to Gordon's eleventh birthday, it is clear that the boy has a visceral dislike for Darrell. Alone together, Nina and Darrell discuss the possibility that Gordon intuits their continuing relationship. They wonder if perhaps Gordon is jealous of Darrell for taking his mother's attention. They agree that Darrell will go away for two years. They kiss farewell, not realizing that young Gordon has returned and sees them. Gordon decides that he will grow up to emulate his namesake, the pilot, to win his mother's love.

On a yacht ten years later, Nina has her three men around her, but she is jealous of her son's fiancée, Madeline. Nina is tempted to reveal Gordon's paternity to her husband, but Sam collapses with a stroke and she vows to protect him. In the final scene several months later, Sam has died. Darrell and Nina get Gordon's blessing to marry, but neither now wishes it. Gordon flies off with Madeline. Nina will marry faithful old Marsden, and her life has come full circle.

The originality of *Strange Interlude*, and its theatrical devices, particularly its length and the spoken asides, made it the subject of numerous articles in the popular and scholarly press. It also spawned many parodies. These included *The Strange Inner Feud* in *The Grand Street Follies of 1928*, a skit in *George White's Scandals*, and even a sequence in the Marx Brothers musical (on stage and screen) *Animal Crackers*. James Thurber got into the action with his "Cross-country Gamut" in *The New Yorker* (February 11, 1928). There was also a parody poem in *The Bookman* (August 1928) and a satire in the *Garrick Gaieties of 1930*. These were among the most immediate evidence that *Strange Interlude* had captured the cultural moment. Because of its length, it is rarely revived, but it stands out among O'Neill's 1920s plays.

Remarkably, O'Neill's next dramatic work, *Mourning Becomes Electra*, easily matched *Strange Interlude* in scope and dramatic experimentation. This five-hour long trilogy was a modern reinvention of Aeschylus' *Oresteia*. It was produced by the Theatre Guild at the Guild Theatre on October 26, 1931, where it ran for 157 performances. Set by O'Neill at the end of the American Civil War, *Mourning Becomes Electra* follows Aeschylus' trilogy structurally. O'Neill divided *Mourning Becomes Electra* into three separate plays. In the first, "Homecoming," O'Neill focuses on Christine Mannon, modeled on Aeschylus' Clytemnestra. Alla Nazimova played the role to critical acclaim. No longer in love with her husband, Ezra Mannon, a general in the Union army and the play's Agamemnon figure, Christine dreads his imminent return from the war. She has indulged in an affair with Mannon's cousin, Captain Adam Brant (Aeschylus' Aegisthus). Brant is a bastard and, as such, has been disowned by the Mannons. Lavinia, the Mannons' twenty-three-year-old daughter and the play's Electra (notably acted by Alice Brady in the original production), has feelings for Brant. This fact deepens her resentment toward Christine. Christine, in turn, has always reserved her love for her son, Orin, the play's Orestes.

When Mannon returns from war, ailing and exhausted, he confronts the duplicitous Christine, who convinces him that she has been faithful. The Mannons spend the night together. But Christine finally confesses her affair with Brant, causing Mannon to suffer a heart attack, with his death brought on as Christine administers poison. She tries to make his sudden demise appear natural, but Lavinia is not fooled, particularly when she finds the discarded poison box. Longing for vengeance, Lavinia is unable to act.

The second play, "The Hunted," begins with Orin's arrival home from the war. He does not want to believe Lavinia's account of events. Christine skillfully manipulates Orin, although he remains haunted by doubts. Locked in complex Freudian relationships, the Mannons find themselves tangled in guilt, desire, and despair. Orin pays respects at his father's bier. When Christine appears, she recoils in horror to see that Lavinia has placed the evidence of her murderous act, the discarded poison box, on Mannon's chest. Now convinced of Christine's guilt, Orin rushes away to kill Brant as O'Neill propels all three characters toward the abyss. Orin's murder of Brant triggers haunted visions of the deaths he observed during the war and within his family. This was a powerful undercurrent for O'Neill and his generation, who reckoned with the horrific death toll of World War I. Unhinged, Orin kills Christine while still longing for her love and forgiveness.

In the final play, "The Haunted," set a year later, O'Neill brings Orin and Lavinia to a full tragic reckoning. Orin shoots himself, unable to face living with his guilt. Lavinia is left to mourn her dead, shutting herself away in the family mansion to live alone for the rest of her life in atonement.

In this harrowing conclusion, O'Neill connects this Americanized Greek tragedy to the deep pains of his own life. These he examined more overtly in his final plays, especially *Long Day's Journey Into Night*, in which he depicts himself, his brother, and his parents bound together in a cycle of despair and mutual recrimination. They are shown as grief-stricken and fated to fail each other and themselves, even in death. *Mourning Becomes Electra* is not without melodramatic elements, but as with *Desire Under the Elms* and *Strange Interlude*, O'Neill achieved tragic depths previously unknown on the American stage.

O'Neill's next major achievement, and perhaps his most surprising work, is the four-act comedy *Ah, Wilderness!* It is a richly imagined, atmospheric portrait of small-town New England life circa 1906. A rose-colored depiction of the world of O'Neill's adolescence, *Ah, Wilderness!* presents family life as O'Neill wished he had known it. It serves as a complement to his other overtly autobiographical play, *Long Day's Journey Into Night*, a tragic portrait of his family set six years after the time of *Ah, Wilderness!* Neither is accurate as autobiography, and

O'Neill seems not to have consciously intended them as complementary. But both reflect the conflicts within O'Neill regarding his family dynamics. These conflicts are at the foundation of many of his plays.

The Theatre Guild produced *Ah, Wilderness!* at the Guild Theatre. It opened on October 2, 1933, for 289 performances. Under the direction of Philip Moeller, *Ah, Wilderness!* was critically applauded as a departure from O'Neill's typically grim tragic voice. Its original star, George M. Cohan, a theatrical legend as an actor, playwright, and songwriter from the era in which the play is set, won accolades for his performance. Cohan played Nat Miller, head of a large family in a small Connecticut town on the Fourth of July weekend of 1906. A genial figure, Nat, along with his wife Essie, wryly observes the bittersweet coming of age of his adolescent son, Richard. Richard is a passionate radical firebrand inflamed by the revolutionary sentiments expressed in contemporary literature. He is in his first love, with Muriel McComber, a classmate. O'Neill contrasts their puppyish coupling with the unhappy relationship of Nat's unmarried sister Lily and Essie's brother, the cherubic drunk Sid Davis. Lily loves Sid, but she cannot accept his irresponsibility and drinking, both of which have recently cost him a job. Sid promises Lily he will behave at the town's Fourth of July picnic if she will go with him to the fireworks that night. When an intoxicated Sid returns from the picnic and makes a shambles of the family dinner, Lily is heartbroken.

O'Neill gently shifts back and forth between the circumstances of Sid and Lily and Richard's romantic travails. Richard's love is complicated when Nat is confronted by McComber, Muriel's narrow-minded father. Her father expresses outrage over racy poetry (Ernest Dowson, Oscar Wilde, Algernon Swinburne) Richard has been sending Muriel. McComber delivers a letter from Muriel stating that she no longer wishes to see Richard, a bit of news that propels him into despair. When an older friend invites Richard to join him for drinks with some "swift babies" at the notorious Pleasant Beach House, the naïve Richard decides he has nothing to lose. He will lead the "pace that kills." He proves no match for Belle, a cynical hustler who exhausts Richard's few dollars on drinks. She then drops him for a better prospect when the money runs out. When a drunken Richard returns home spouting speeches from Henrik Ibsen's *Hedda Gabler*, Nat and Essie worry over what might have transpired at the "low dive." The next day it becomes clear that Richard has only overindulged in alcohol. Nat steels himself to explain the facts of life, which he does in a bumbling, embarrassed — albeit loving — way.

Then Richard learns that Mr. McComber forced Muriel to break off their relationship. In an act of defiance that impresses him, she is waiting to meet him at the beach. In the moonlight they express undying devotion sealed by a first gentle kiss. As the evening draws to a close, Lily and Sid painfully reconcile. A rueful Nat observes that the two will never find the happiness he and Essie recognize as their particular good fortune. As they watch Richard gazing up at the moonlight, Nat wistfully reflects on the passage of time and the enduring power of love.

O'Neill planned a darker sequel to *Ah, Wilderness!* It was to be set in the aftermath of World War I, in which an embittered Nat is unable to cope with a rapidly changing world. Meanwhile, Richard, returning from the war, grapples with profound emotional and physical scars. O'Neill never completed this sequel, but an outline of its plot was found among his papers.

Despite the critical successes of *Strange Interlude* and *Mourning Becomes Electra*, and the popular success of the long-running *Ah, Wilderness!*, the second phase of O'Neill's playwriting career began a precipitous decline. It perhaps began with the disappointments of *Marco Millions*, *Lazarus Laughed*, and *Dynamo*. With the flop of *Days Without End* in 1934, O'Neill, without fanfare, withdrew from active production of further work (except for disappointing productions of *The Iceman Cometh* in 1946 and *A Moon for the Misbegotten* in 1947). He had hopes of completing his planned eleven-play cycle, *A Tale of Possessors Self-Dispossessed*. He was also planning a companion one-act cycle,

By Way of Obit. These ambitious projects were the center of the third and final phase of O'Neill's playwriting career. Their development was hampered by O'Neill's personal issues and increasing health problems, along with a few deeply personal dramas.

WORK: STAGE THREE (1935–1943)

Ironically, O'Neill's critical reputation was at its lowest ebb during the years in which he was actually writing what are now considered his finest and most important plays. At the time of his death in 1953, O'Neill was thought of, if at all, as an artifact of the American theatrical past. It was also believed that his best plays had been written during the 1920s. Other serious dramatists began to predominate during the 1930s and 1940s. Maxwell Anderson, Robert E. Sherwood, Thornton Wilder, Clifford Odets, Tennessee Williams, and Arthur Miller began taking American drama in new directions.

Dismissive attitudes about O'Neill's significance were radically reconsidered beginning in 1956 with the widely acclaimed premiere posthumous production of *Long Day's Journey Into Night*. This inspired a critical reevaluation of his achievement. It was further aided by a series of critically appreciated revivals of his earlier works as well as the late plays on which much of his towering international reputation is now based. Widely regarded as America's foremost dramatist, O'Neill's predominance has only been challenged by the accomplishments of Tennessee Williams. Williams acknowledged his debt to O'Neill as the Prometheus of serious American drama.

O'Neill's increasing health problems, including a pronounced tremor in his hands, made the act of writing difficult. Even so, during the late 1930s O'Neill worked on the plays for the two planned cycles. Of the cycle *A Tale of Possessors Self-Dispossessed*, only a final draft of *A Touch of the Poet* and an early six-hour-long draft of *More Stately Mansions* survive. For the one-act cycle, *By Way of Obit*, only the completed *Hughie* survives. O'Neill accomplished much work for both cycles.

Unfortunately, not long before his death, O'Neill destroyed manuscripts and notes for the plays. He did this in despair over his inability to work. He was also fearful that others would attempt to complete work that he regarded as less than fully formed. This sad turn of events is somewhat mitigated by the fact that O'Neill completed three other major plays. These were *The Iceman Cometh* in 1939, *Long Day's Journey Into Night* in 1941, and *A Moon for the Misbegotten* in 1943. These, as well as *A Touch of the Poet* and *Hughie*, significantly enhanced his reputation when they were produced in the 1950s, 1960s, and 1970s. By this time, O'Neill was widely acknowledged as America's greatest playwright.

A central theme of *The Iceman Cometh* centers on the human need for illusions. Hickey, the traveling salesman and protagonist of the play, makes this clear when he attempts to awaken his friends, the denizens of Harry Hope's saloon, from their illusions. "I meant it when I say I hope today will be the biggest day in your life," Hickey tells them, "and in the lives of everyone here, the beginning of a new life of peace and contentment where no pipe dreams can ever nag at you again." In his attempt to strip his friends of their illusions, Hickey tragically comes to understand their necessity. The isolating modern world is represented by the empty place Hope's saloon symbolizes. It is an existential haven for the damaged and lost souls, not unlike the characters found in the plays of Samuel Beckett, who face a bleak world with an uncomprehending sense of their place in it. They are left with only an aching sense of loss and fear of what is to come.

The Iceman Cometh was the last O'Neill play performed on Broadway during his lifetime. Reclusive and ailing, O'Neill completed the play in 1939, but it was not produced until October 9, 1946. It opened at the Martin Beck Theatre for a disappointingly short run. Reviewers found the lengthy play inferior to O'Neill's earlier achievements. This was principally because of weaknesses in the production, particularly the performance of James Barton as Hickey. Critical rejection and audience apathy obscured its merits until an acclaimed 1956 revival at New York's Circle in the Square Theatre. Since then, *The Iceman*

Cometh has come to be regarded as an O'Neill masterpiece, and it is frequently revived. Most recently, in 1999, Kevin Spacey starred in a limited Broadway run. It was filmed twice, for television in 1960 (based on the 1956 revival) and in 1973. O'Neill's setting of Harry Hope's "last chance" saloon in New York City in the summer of 1912 is a fictionalized reflection of Jimmy-the-Priest's. This was the barroom O'Neill frequented during that same year, when, submerged in alcohol and drug abuse, he nearly succeeded in committing suicide. His life changed that year, when he was diagnosed with tuberculosis and while recovering determined to become a playwright. Significantly, *The Iceman Cometh* and *Long Day's Journey Into Night* are both set in that watershed year. As the end of his life neared, O'Neill returned to the eventful start of his adult life.

The down-and-out habitués of Harry Hope's bar delude themselves about their past failings and the possibility of restoring lost fortunes, relationships, dreams, and shattered confidence. In the meantime, they drink themselves into oblivion. They are aroused only by the imminent arrival of Theodore Hickman, known to all as "Hickey," a fifty-year-old hardware salesman, who regales them with tall stories and buys endless rounds of drinks whenever he happens to visit. Hickey, a carousing, boozing braggart, has always bolstered the spirits of the lost souls at Hope's gin mill, but this time Hickey is not his usual jocular self. Instead, he is filled with a missionary's zeal in forcing them all to face the hard truths of their lives. Each clings to an illusion representing some facet of life's experience. O'Neill imbues them with everything from romantic dreams to familial betrayals and political disillusionments. Their illusions are, as Hickey insists, burdens preventing them from finding contentment. He pressures each to do what they continually claim they will one day do — to act on their "pipe dreams," to face their individual truth. Hickey tells them that their illusions of hope are "the things that really poison and ruin a guy's life and keep him from finding peace. If you knew how free and contented I feel now. I'm like a new man."

Despite this, Hickey's goal backfires as each of the derelicts tumbles into confusion and despair as their particular pipe dream is proven to be no more than a lie. There is no hope for any of them, and this crushing realization is more than they are able to bear. They sink into a "half-dead" state in which even booze fails to bring the false peace of alcoholic oblivion. Hickey is shocked by this disquieting gloom, and he shouts, "By rights you should be contented now, without a single damned hope or lying dream left to torment you!" Slowly it dawns on him that the "remorse and guilt" he intended to liberate them from has only served to plunge them into hopeless despair.

The illusions of the barflies are subsequently restored by the spectacle of Hickey facing his own. He has taken action in his own life, and the results are horrifying. He has told the barflies often of Evelyn, his loving, forgiving wife. Now Hickey relates the true unhappy tale of their marriage. Evelyn has repeatedly forgiven his numerous lapses with alcohol and with other women, which has built up a deep resentment in him. "I began to be afraid I was going bughouse," he admits, "because sometimes I couldn't forgive her for forgiving me. I even caught myself hating her for making me hate myself so much. There's a limit to the guilt you can feel and the forgiveness and pity you can take!" The unhappy Evelyn has indulged in a sad affair with the iceman, an act that has destroyed Hickey's illusion of her perfection. He has even suggested in the past that she find happiness elsewhere. When she actually does so, he hypocritically cannot forgive her, although he claims to understand. According to Hickey, Evelyn continues to love him and forgive his transgressions. Wracked by guilt, Hickey insists he needed to spare her further distress: "The last night I'd driven myself crazy trying to figure some way out for her. I went in the bedroom. I was going to tell her it was the end. But I couldn't do that to her. She was sound asleep. I thought, God, if she'd only never wake up, she'd never know! And then it came to me — the only possible way out, for her sake. I remembered I'd given her a gun for protection while I was away and it was in the bureau drawer. She'd never feel any pain, never wake up from her dream." The drunks recoil, but Harry Hope, mired in his own despair, angrily shouts, "You married her, and you caught her cheating with the iceman, and you croaked her, and who the hell cares?"

As detectives arrive to arrest him, Hickey realizes that "pipe dreams" are the only escape from the brutalizing realities of life as he clings to his belief that he killed Evelyn only to spare her pain. He is dragged off to prison, and Hope and the others return to their drinking and dreaming.

The Iceman Cometh undoubtedly seemed too hopeless in outlook for Broadway audiences in the immediate aftermath of World War II. American soldiers were returning home to unprecedented economic opportunity and to marriages, creating a "baby boom." Technological progress was also greatly enhancing the overall quality of life. It was a period of conformity and optimism, and O'Neill's blunt assessment of the cultural landscape seemed out of step. Audiences and critics alike were not adequately prepared for the stark tragedy of this and O'Neill's other final plays. *A Moon for the Misbegotten* (1943) closed during its out-of-town tryout in 1947. Like *The Iceman Cometh*, *A Moon for the Misbegotten* has since won critical praise as a complement to O'Neill's semi-autobiographical masterpiece, *Long Day's Journey Into Night*.

A Moon for the Misbegotten continues the story of the character of James "Jamie" Tyrone Jr. in *Long Day's Journey Into Night*. He is a dramatic alter ego for O'Neill's alcoholic brother, James "Jamie" O'Neill Jr. Unfortunately, the play's other central character, Irish farm girl Josie Hogan, has often proven to be a casting challenge even though some celebrated actresses — Colleen Dewhurst and Cherry Jones, for example — have been memorable in the role despite falling short of O'Neill's description of a woman as physically powerful as a man, yet beautiful. Josie is a powerful woman who emerges as a Madonna figure, described by Harold Clurman as "of the earth, warm and hearty." Josie embodies aspects of many women O'Neill created in earlier works. She is a mixture of maternal and carnal impulses drawn from

O'Neill's complicated feelings for his mother and wives, as well as his interest in Sigmund Freud's psychological theories. Josie is a cruder, more rural embodiment of themes found in other plays. O'Neill explored these through such women characters as Abigail Putnam in *Desire Under the Elms*, Nina Leeds in *Strange Interlude*, and both Christine and Lavinia Mannon in *Mourning Becomes Electra*.

A Moon for the Misbegotten is a static play set outside a rundown Connecticut farmhouse owned by Jamie Tyrone and run by a boozy, two-fisted Irish tenant, Phil Hogan. It begins in September 1923 as Hogan's son, Mike, flees the deprivations of the farm and his father's harsh demands. Mike is briefly interrupted in his departure by his twenty-eight-year-old sister, Josie. She is a woman so large "that she is almost a freak — five feet eleven in her stockings and weighs around one hundred and eighty." Josie is powerfully strong, as demonstrated when she manhandles both her brother and father. Yet "there is no mannish quality about her" and her Irish heritage "is stamped on her face [. . .] It is not a pretty face, but her large dark-blue eyes give it a note of beauty, and her smile, revealing even white teeth, gives it charm."

Josie secretly loves Jamie, whom she calls Jim. She adopts a coarse, sluttish manner as a protective shield for her vulnerabilities. Jim is recently returned from a disastrous train trip bringing home the body of his mother for burial. In a distressed, drunken state, he spent the night with a prostitute on the train. This act of disrespect fills him with guilt, and he seeks comfort from Josie. Jim's Irish charm reveals "a style set by well-groomed Broadway gamblers who would like to be mistaken for Wall Street brokers." This manner keeps him attractive to the opposite sex. Josie finds him appealing despite the swagger. Jim takes "sardonic relish" in bantering with Hogan and Josie, although his gibes occasionally hurt Josie. The tone of their relationship is established as he rises when she appears, triggering her reply, "Don't get up. Sure, you know I'm no lady." Josie's pose of a tough woman who has known many men does not fool Jim. He vacillates between enjoying her pose and resenting it. "For God's sake, cut out that kind of talk, Josie. It sounds like hell," he insists. He understands that Josie is a virgin, a fact she is as ashamed of as other women might be of a lack of virtue.

Surprisingly, O'Neill adopts an almost farcical tone in the first two acts of *A Moon for the Misbegotten*. Josie and Hogan indulge in wisecracks and a raucous encounter with the neighboring oil millionaire, Harder, who wants to buy the farm to be rid of them. The comedy masks the serious dilemma faced by Josie and Hogan. They both fear that Jamie's irresponsible drinking may lead him to make the sale, although Josie is more concerned with Jamie's well-being and her feelings of love for him. The air of doom about him suggests he is in search of something else. His need is foreshadowed by a wisecrack he makes to the solicitous Josie, "That's right. Mother me, Josie. I love it." Seeking forgiveness from a mother who can longer give it, Jamie turns Josie into a surrogate.

Josie hopes that Jim will stay sober and keep a planned date with her. She is hurt to learn that he is drunk and seems to have made a deal to sell the farm. Angered as well, she decides to get even. Hogan, protective of his daughter's feelings, denies her self-deprecation. The compassionate Josie is softened when Jim arrives in a miserable state. They settle down in the moonlight with a bottle of Hogan's whiskey as she feigns jealousy over Jim's other women. "You're a fool to be jealous of anyone," he insists. "You're the only woman I care a damn about." Josie is moved, even more so when she realizes that Jim has kept his promise and not sold the farm. She reverts to her "brazen-trollop act" attempting to josh Jim out of his hurt that she has not trusted him: "Are you going to keep that up — with me? [. . .] You can take the truth, Josie — from me. Because you and I belong to the same club. We can kid the world but we can't fool ourselves."

Josie hopes they can spend a loving night together. Unfortunately, when the alcohol releases Jim's drunken "cynical lust," Josie is frightened and repulsed. Awakened from this momentary blackout, Jim is remorseful. He tells her that she "ought to thank me for letting you see," for he is convinced that he is too far gone and that any future for them would be "a million times worse." He wants only to fall asleep in her arms. But a deeper alcoholic blackout causes him to recount, in heart-wrenching detail, the train trip home with his mother's body. Josie is horrified, but understands that she has the power to assuage his guilt. "I understand now, Jim, darling," she tells him, "and I'm proud you came to me as the one in the world you know loves you enough to understand and forgive — and I do forgive!" Jim falls asleep while Josie holds him, finding dark humor in her situation: "God forgive me, it's a fine end to all my scheming, to sit here with the dead hugged to my breast, and the silly mug of the moon grinning down, enjoying the joke!" The relief she has brought Jim has come at the cost of her own hopes, for their love will never be consummated. Josie knows she has brought him comfort on his lonely path to death. When Jim departs in the morning, Josie bids him farewell: "May you have your wish and die in your sleep, soon, Jim, darling. May you rest forever in forgiveness and peace."

The Connecticut setting of the elegiac *A Moon for the Misbegotten* was a familiar one to O'Neill. He spent part of his youth in New London, Connecticut, the unnamed locale of the play. As in prior work, both classical theater and trends in modernist drama inspired O'Neill. However, O'Neill abandoned overt use of these inspirations in *A Moon for the Misbegotten.* That was also true in his last plays, including *The Iceman Cometh* and *Long Day's Journey Into Night.*

Long Day's Journey Into Night, like *The Iceman Cometh* and *A Moon for the Misbegotten*, is stripped of obvious theatrical artifice. These are works in which O'Neill stares unblinking into the existential abyss of an isolating, hope-starved century. He also looks at the deep regrets and haunted memories of his own life. Harold Bloom refers to *Long Day's Journey Into Night* as O'Neill's "masterpiece." He calls it the "best play in our more than two centuries as a nation." Bloom is hardly alone in this opinion. As a literary critic, Bloom finds fault with O'Neill's "limitations." But he acknowledges that O'Neill compels readers to "revise our notions of just how strictly literary an art drama necessarily has to be." In this, Bloom hits on the essential conundrum of O'Neill the dramatist. Production choices made in staging his plays often troubled O'Neill. His frustration with the transition from page to stage is evident in the "literary" quality he brings to his plays. The plays often read as well as they play. Stage directions, character descriptions, indications of attitudes and emotions for the characters are carefully written. They are as carefully done as any line of dialogue in O'Neill's oeuvre. He attempts to leave nothing to chance. He was surely aware that those producing his works would not ultimately feel bound by these directions. Bloom believes the effective use of stage directions in O'Neill's plays came from his admiration of August Strindberg. However, it seems more likely that O'Neill had so fully realized his greatest plays in his head that he was compelled to "stage" them himself, if only in his imagination. He captured these imagined productions in the careful descriptions in his stage directions.

The heartbroken O'Neill paints in words a heartbreaking family portrait in *Long Day's Journey Into Night*. It is, as Bloom notes, a result of O'Neill's "Nietzschean realization that the truly memorable is always associated with what is most painful." In the twentieth century — and on into the twenty-first — family, and an individual's relation to it, has been the central vehicle in American drama for exploration of life's most profound personal struggles. In O'Neill's own case, in his first full-length play, *Beyond the Horizon*, the model is established. It is continued through *Long Day's Journey Into Night*.

O'Neill's plays are followed by the greatest plays of his immediate successors. These include Thornton Wilder (*Our Town, The Skin of Our Teeth*), Tennessee Williams (*The Glass Menagerie, A Streetcar Named Desire*), and Arthur Miller (*All My Sons, Death of a Salesman*). Others have come after, from Edward Albee (*Who's Afraid of Virginia Woolf?, A Delicate Balance*) to Tracy Letts (*Killer Joe, August: Osage County*). Joy and despair, hope and disillusion, faith and betrayal, optimism and disappointment, loss and rebirth, addiction and violence are all human emotions most vividly portrayed within the confines of family life. This is true however extended a family may be in post-modern American theater. As Bloom writes, O'Neill's "strength was neither in stance nor style, but in the dramatic representation of illusions and despairs, in the persuasive imitation of human personality, particularly in its self-destructive weakness."

Illusion and despair are at the center of the lives of the Tyrone family in *Long Day's Journey Into Night*. The Tyrones are among the most compelling characters in the canon of American dramatic literature. The four Tyrones are loosely based on O'Neill's parents, James and Mary Ellen "Ella" Quinlan O'Neill, and his elder brother, Jamie. O'Neill's stage alter ego, Edmund, is named for his brother who died in infancy. As such, the play is the fullest realization of O'Neill's autobiographical proclivities, although much of the play is fiction. It also works with the recurrent themes of the final phase of his work as a dramatist. This four-act play was neither published nor produced until three years after O'Neill's 1953 death. This occurred even though in his will it was his stated desire that this intense, deeply personal drama be held back from publication until twenty-five years after his passing and never produced.

In O'Neill's later plays, as in this grim, realistic family tragedy, O'Neill abandoned the bold experimentation of his plays of the 1920s and early 30s. Instead he focused intently on the complexities and contradictions within the psyches of his central characters, the "four haunted Tyrones." This is a stark, unrelenting exorcism of his own family's dynamics, but it is woven with compassion by a playwright at the peak of his estimable abilities. *Long Day's Journey Into Night* is set in the summer of 1912. It focuses on celebrated romantic actor James Tyrone; his wife, Mary; and their adult sons, Jamie and Edmund. Summering at the family's modest Connecticut cottage, Mary is convalescing from a battle with morphine addiction that began when she gave birth to Edmund. The men exude hope that Mary is finally free of drugs, which have been the source of a long family nightmare that has deeply affected all of them. However, Mary's precarious "recovery" is threatened by the illness of Edmund. He has been unable to shake what she stubbornly refers to as a "summer cold." Nervously awaiting results of medical tests, the men are ruefully convinced that Edmund has tuberculosis. They endeavor to keep the truth from Mary for as long as possible. Mary's deep fears for Edmund, coupled with the demons of her own life, slowly erode her resolve. To escape her profound fears, she secretly begins taking morphine again as the men continue to hope. As the agonizing day wears on, James, Jamie, and Edmund realize that their hopes for Mary are dashed. They sink into alcoholic despair and a cycle of guilt, accusations, and misery. "I'd begun to hope, if she'd beaten the game, I could, too," cries Jamie as the sad day journeys into night.

Jamie is an alcoholic wastrel in the best of times. He seems to be the protector of his younger brother, concerning himself with Edmund's alcohol intake and urging him toward literary success. At a climactic moment, O'Neill allows Jamie, in a drunken state, to express the twisted nature of his love. Deeply ashamed and despairing, Jamie warns Edmund "against me. Mama and Papa are right. I've been a rotten bad influence. And worst of it is, I did it on purpose. [. . .] Did it on purpose to make a bum of you. Or part of me did. A big part."

The paradoxes of sibling love and uneasy relations within the family unit are often evident in O'Neill's depiction of stage siblings. Beginning with his first full-length drama, the Pulitzer Prize–winning *Beyond the Horizon* (1920), he subsequently continued his dramatic portrait of his own brother in *A Moon for the Misbegotten*. This is O'Neill's final play, set eleven years after the events of *Long Day's Journey Into Night*, as Jamie is drinking himself to death following the death of their mother. O'Neill's agonized depictions of his mother and brother are matched by his conflicted vision of his father, whose destructive miserliness derives from a desperately poverty-stricken childhood that has imprinted deep fears on the old man. Tyrone regretfully reconsiders his stage career, which has brought lucrative rewards thanks to a popular melodramatic hit (*The Count of Monte Cristo*, in O'Neill's real father's case). Unfortunately, the lack of artistic challenge cost him a more spiritually rewarding career as a Shakespearean actor.

O'Neill's own self portrait in *Long Day's Journey Into Night* highlights his deep feelings of isolation from his family — and from the world in general. These feelings tormented him throughout his life. The complex web of love and estrangement O'Neill experienced in his relationships with his parents and brother were largely replicated in his marriages and with his children. His first brief marriage, to Kathleen Jenkins, had little impact on him since they were almost never together. The marriage produced a son, Eugene O'Neill Jr., who, curiously, was the only of his children O'Neill developed much of a relationship with after their childhoods.

His second marriage, to writer Agnes Boulton, lasted nearly a decade and produced two children, Shane and Oona. Despite the fact that both O'Neill and Boulton were writers, the marriage fractured. This was largely a result of O'Neill's bouts of drinking, the demands of his work once he had achieved his first successes, and his deep-seated fear that traditional family life would draw him away from his dramatic ambitions. The marriage ended when O'Neill became involved with Carlotta Monterey, who became his third wife. His children remained with Boulton and rarely saw their father. When, as an eighteen-year-old, Oona married the forty-something actor Charlie Chaplin, O'Neill would never speak to her again. Shane's addictions to alcohol and drugs (not unlike O'Neill's own) largely terminated his relationship with his father.

Although O'Neill's marriage to Carlotta lasted for twenty-five years, until his death, there were periodic estrangements. This was particularly true when illness hampered both after World War II. In all of his familial relations, O'Neill placed the needs of wives and children well below his work. He also seemed to project the estrangement he had felt in his parents' home into his own. He was isolated in his own skin. At one point in *Long Day's Journey Into Night*, this is explained by Edmund, his dramatic alter ego. He says, "It was a great mistake, my being born a man, I would have been much more successful as a sea gull or a fish. As it is, I will always be a stranger who never feels at home, who does not want and is not really wanted, who can never belong, who must always be a little in love with death!" As *Long Day's Journey Into Night* concludes, Mary is lost in a drug-induced fog, wandering the cottage dragging her wedding dress, the symbol of her faded illusions, behind her. Edmund, who is indeed suffering from tuberculosis, must leave for a sanitarium. James and Jamie sink into alcoholic despondency over Edmund's uncertain future and bitter disappointment over Mary's seemingly unconquerable addiction and their failure to save her.

Jose Quintero directed the original 1956 Broadway production. It featured Fredric March as Tyrone, Florence Eldridge as Mary, Jason Robards Jr. as Jamie, and Bradford Dillman as Edmund. It reaped a posthumous Pulitzer Prize for O'Neill (his fourth). This initiated a critical reassessment of his work. Indeed, after years of neglect, his reputation was restored by this production. It began many revivals of his plays, insuring his predominance among twentieth-century American playwrights. *Long Day's Journey Into Night* has won recognition as O'Neill's greatest achievement. It is frequently revived, including a notable British production in 1971 starring Laurence Olivier as Tyrone and Constance Cummings as Mary (subsequently filmed for television in 1973). An acclaimed 1962 screen version featured Ralph Richardson, Katharine Hepburn, Dean Stockwell, and Robards reprising his acclaimed performance as Jamie. Robards also appeared in a 1988 revival as Tyrone, costarring with Colleen Dewhurst as Mary. An all-black cast starring Earle Hyman as Tyrone and Ruby Dee as Mary was filmed for television in 1982. A Broadway revival in 1986 starred Jack Lemmon as Tyrone and Kevin Spacey as Jamie. More recently, a 2003 revival brought critical accolades to Vanessa Redgrave as Mary, co-starring with Brian Dennehy as Tyrone, Philip Seymour Hoffman as Jamie, and Robert Sean Leonard as Edmund.

Following the completion of these last plays, O'Neill's last decade of life was filled with disappointments in his work (the failures of *The Iceman Cometh* and *A Moon for the Misbegotten* in production). He also experienced unhappiness in his personal life, with a troubled relationship with Carlotta Monterey and fraught relationships with his children, including the suicide death of his eldest son, Eugene Jr., in 1950. The struggles might have been surmounted if not coupled with O'Neill's physical decline. His tremor worsened, and other health problems prevented work or even the enjoyment of life's pleasures. Near the end of his life, he destroyed incomplete work, particularly the materials related to his two planned cycles of plays. He also withheld his work from production. Unfortunately, he withdrew from friends and family members. He died in 1953 in a Boston hotel room, acknowledging the irony of having also been born in one. He had little awareness that his creative reputation would only grow after his death.

Within just a few years following his death, O'Neill's reputation soared to new heights from the low ebb of his last years. He emerged with an image as the greatest American dramatist. He is challenged only by Tennessee Williams in both quality and quantity of achievement. The 1956 premiere of O'Neill's *Long Day's Journey Into Night* on Broadway began an O'Neill renaissance that has not abated in over fifty years. Each revival of his greatest works only seems to enhance their luster. Productions of his lesser-known or misunderstood plays bring new respect and reassessment.

No American playwright has achieved the international acclaim O'Neill's works have brought him. Scholarly attention and critical acclaim for his achievement grow with each passing year. Despite the fact that the often grim and tragic nature of his dramas seems counter to America's optimism, O'Neill provided through his vast output of plays an alternate portrait of a country that has yet to achieve its own high ideals. As such, his work can be seen as offering a profound optimism. He suggests that despite its many failings, a great nation, like a family, may one day live up to its ideals.

DRAMATIC MOMENTS

from the Early Plays

These short excerpts are from the playwright's early plays. They give a taste of the work of the playwright. Each has a short introduction in brackets that helps the reader understand the context of the excerpt. The excerpts, which are in chronological order, illustrate the main themes mentioned in the In an Hour essay. Premiere date is given.

from **Beyond the Horizon** (1918)
from Act One

CHARACTERS

Robert

Ruth

Andrew

[The first full-length play of Eugene O'Neill's produced on Broadway, where it won the Pulitzer Prize for Drama in 1920, *Beyond the Horizon* features the first important O'Neill protagonist, Robert "Rob" Mayo, a dreamy poet, who longs to escape rural New England to see the world, in contrast with his brother, Andrew, who is eager to manage the family farm and marry Ruth, his childhood sweetheart. In the first act, Rob reveals himself to Ruth, who is bethrothed to Andrew.]

ROBERT: Those were the only happy moments in my life then, dreaming there at that window. I liked to be all alone — those times. I got to know all the different kinds of sunsets by heart. And all those sunsets took place over there — *(He points.)* beyond the horizon. So gradually I came to believe that all the wonders of the world happened on the other side of those hills. There was the home of the good fairies who performed beautiful miracles. I believed in fairies then. *(With a smile.)* Perhaps I still do believe in them. Anyway, in those days they were real enough, and sometimes I could actually hear them calling to me to come out and play with them, dance with them down the road in the dusk in a game of hide-and-seek to find out where the sun was hiding himself. They sang their little songs to me, songs that told of all the wonderful things they had in their home on the other side of the hills; and they promised to show me all of them, if I'd only come, come! But I couldn't come then, and I used to cry sometimes and Ma would think I was in pain. *(He breaks off suddenly with a laugh.)* That's why I'm going now, I suppose. For I can still hear them calling. But the horizon is as far away and as luring as ever. *(He turns to her — softly.)* Do you understand now, Ruth?

RUTH: *(Spellbound, in a whisper.)* Yes.

ROBERT: You feel it then?

RUTH: Yes, yes, I do! *(Unconsciously she snuggles close against his side. His arm steals about her as if they were not aware of the action.)* Oh, Rob, how could I help feeling it? You tell things so beautifully!

ROBERT: *(Suddenly realizing his arm is around her, and that her head is resting against his shoulder, gently takes his arm away. Ruth, brought back to herself, is overcome with confusion.)* So now you know why I'm going. It's for that reason — that and one other.

RUTH: You've another? Then you must tell me that, too.

ROBERT: *(Looking at her searchingly. She drops her eyes before his gaze.)* I wonder if I ought to! You'll promise not to be angry — whatever it is?

RUTH: *(Softly, her face still averted.)* Yes, I promise.

ROBERT: *(Simply.)* I love you. That's the other reason.

RUTH: *(Hiding her face in her hands.)* Oh, Rob!

ROBERT: I wasn't going to tell you, but I feel I have to. It can't matter now that I'm going so far away, and for so long — perhaps forever. I've loved you all these years, but the realization never came 'til I agreed to go away with Uncle Dick. Then I thought of leaving you, and the pain of that thought revealed to me in a little flash — that I loved you, had loved you as long as I could remember. *(He gently pulls one of Ruth's hands away from her face.)* You mustn't mind my telling you this, Ruth. I realize how impossible it all is — and I understand; for the revelation of my own love seemed to open my eyes to the love of others. I saw Andy's love for you — and I know that you must love him.

RUTH: *(Breaking out stormily.)* I don't! I don't love Andy! I don't! *(Robert stares at her in stupid astonishment. Ruth weeps hysterically.)* Whatever — put such a fool notion into — into your head? *(She suddenly throws her arms about his neck and hides her head on his shoulder.)* Oh, Rob!

Don't go away! Please! You mustn't, now! You can't! I won't let you! It'd break my — my heart!

ROBERT: *(The expression of stupid bewilderment giving way to one of over-whelming joy. He presses her close to him — slowly and tenderly.)* Do you mean that — that you love me?

RUTH: *(Sobbing.)* Yes, yes — of course I do — what d'you s'pose? *(She lifts her head and looks into his eyes with a tremulous smile.)* You stupid thing! *(He kisses her.)* I've loved you right along.

ROBERT: *(Mystified.)* But you and Andy were always together!

RUTH: Because you never seemed to want to go any place with me. You were always reading an old book, and not paying any attention to me. I was too proud to let you see I cared because I thought the year you had away to college had made you stuck-up, and you thought yourself too educated to waste any time on me.

ROBERT: *(Kissing her.)* And I was thinking — *(With a laugh.)* What fools we've both been!

RUTH: *(Overcome by a sudden fear.)* You won't go away on the trip, will you, Rob? You'll tell them you can't go on account of me, won't you? You can't go now! You can't!

ROBERT: *(Bewildered.)* Perhaps — you can come too.

RUTH: Oh, Rob, don't be so foolish. You know I can't. Who'd take care of Ma? Don't you see I couldn't go — on her account? *(She clings to him imploringly.)* Please don't go — not now. Tell them you've decided not to. They won't mind. I know your mother and father'll be glad. They'll all be. They don't want you to go so far away from them. Please, Rob! We'll be so happy here together where it's natural and we know things. Please tell me you won't go!

ROBERT: *(Face to face with a definite, final decision, betrays the conflict going on within him.)* But — Ruth — I — Uncle Dick —

RUTH: He won't mind when he knows it's for your happiness to stay. How could he? *(As Robert remains silent she bursts into sobs again.)* Oh, Rob! And you said — you loved me!

ROBERT: *(Conquered by this appeal — an irrevocable decision in his voice.)*

I won't go, Ruth. I promise you. There! Don't cry! *(He presses her to him, stroking her hair tenderly. After a pause he speaks with happy hopefulness.)* Perhaps after all Andy was right — righter than he knew — when he said I could find all the things I was seeking for here, at home on the farm. I think love must have been the secret — the secret that called to me from over the world's rim — the secret beyond every horizon; and when I did not come, it came to me. *(He clasps Ruth to him fiercely.)* Oh, Ruth, our love is sweeter than any distant dream! *(He kisses her passionately and steps to the ground, lifting Ruth in his arms and carrying her to the road where he puts her down.)*

RUTH: *(With a happy laugh.)* My, but you're strong!

ROBERT: Come! We'll go tell them at once.

RUTH: *(Dismayed.)* Oh, no, don't, Rob, not 'til after I've gone. There'd be bound to be such a scene with them all together.

ROBERT: *(Kissing her — gaily.)* As you like — little Miss Common Sense!

RUTH: Let's go, then. *(She takes his hand, and they start to go off left. Robert suddenly stops and turns as though for a last look at the hills and the dying sunset flush.)*

ROBERT: *(Looking upward and pointing.)* See! The first star. *(He bends down and kisses her tenderly.)* Our star!

RUTH: *(In a soft murmur.)* Yes. Our very own star. *(They stand for a moment looking up at it, their arms around each other. Then Ruth takes his hand again and starts to lead him away.)* Come, Rob, let's go. *(His eyes are fixed again on the horizon as he half turns to follow her. Ruth urges.)* We'll be late for supper, Rob.

ROBERT: *(Shakes his head impatiently, as though he were throwing off some disturbing thought — with a laugh.)* All right. We'll run then. Come on! *(They run off laughing as the curtain falls.)*

CURTAIN

from **Beyond the Horizon** (1918)

from Act Three

CHARACTERS

Andrew

Robert

[Andrew's devastated reaction to the love of Robert and Ruth causes him to leave the farm. With this trading of destinies, the brothers proceed with their lives. As the years roll by, Robert takes charge of the farm, but fails as a farmer. He realizes he has not been true to his destiny and falls into despair. In the final scene of *Beyond the Horizon*, Andrew has returned, and the old confusions in the relationships among Robert, Ruth, and Andrew are revived. Robert is dying and frustrated by his failure with the farm, which he has come to despise.]

ANDREW: *(Stopping and looking about him.)* There he is! I knew it! I knew we'd find him here.

ROBERT: *(Trying to raise himself to a sitting position as they hasten to his side — with a wan smile.)* I thought I'd given you the slip.

ANDREW: *(With kindly bullying.)* Well you didn't, you old scoundrel, and we're going to take you right back where you belong — in bed. *(He makes a motion to lift Robert.)*

ROBERT: Don't, Andy. Don't I tell you!

ANDREW: You're in pain?

ROBERT: *(Simply.)* No. I'm dying. *(He falls back weakly. Ruth sinks down beside him with a sob and pillows his head on her lap. Andrew stands looking down at him helplessly. Robert moves his head restlessly on Ruth's lap.)* I couldn't stand it back there in the room. It seemed as if all my life — I've been cooped in a room. So I thought I'd try to end as I might have — if I'd had the courage — alone — in a ditch by the open road — watching the sun rise.

ANDREW: Rob! Don't talk. You're wasting your strength. Rest a while and then we'll carry you —

ROBERT: Still hoping, Andy? Don't. I know. *(There is a pause during which he breathes heavily, straining his eyes toward the horizon.)* The sun comes so slowly. *(With an ironical smile.)* The doctor told me to go to the far-off places — and I'd be cured. He was right. That was always the cure for me. It's too late — for this life — but — *(He has a fit of coughing which racks his body.)*

ANDREW: *(With a hoarse sob.)* Rob! *(He clenches his fists in an impotent rage against fate.)* God! God! *(Ruth sobs brokenly and wipes Robert's lips with her handkerchief.)*

ROBERT: *(In a voice which is suddenly ringing with the happiness of hope.)* You mustn't feel sorry for me. Don't you see I'm happy at last — free — free! — freed from the farm — free to wander on and on — eternally! *(He raises himself on his elbow, his face radiant, and points to the horizon.)* Look! Isn't it beautiful beyond the hills? I can hear the old voices calling me to come — *(Exultantly.)* And this time I'm going! It isn't the end. It's a free beginning — the start of my voyage! I've won to my trip — the right of release — beyond the horizon! Oh, you ought to be glad — glad — for my sake! *(He collapses weakly.)* Andy! *(Andrew bends down to him.)* Remember Ruth —

ANDREW: I'll take care of her, I swear to you, Rob!

ROBERT: Ruth has suffered — remember, Andy — only through sacrifice — the secret beyond there — *(He suddenly raises himself with his last remaining strength and points to the horizon where the edge of the sun's disc is rising from the rim of the hills.)* The sun! *(He remains with his eyes fixed on it for a moment. A rattling noises throbs from his throat. He mumbles.)* Remember! *(And falls back and is still. Ruth gives a cry of horror and springs to her feet, shuddering, her hands over her eyes. Andrew bends on one knee beside the body, placing a hand over Robert's heart, then he kisses his brother reverentially on the forehead and stands up.)*

ANDREW: *(Facing Ruth, the body between them — in a dead voice.)* He's dead. *(With a sudden burst of fury.)* God damn you, you never told him!

RUTH: *(Piteously.)* He was so happy without my lying to him.

ANDREW: *(Pointing to the body — trembling with the violence of his rage.)* This is your doing, you damn woman, you coward, you murderess!

RUTH: *(Sobbing.)* Don't, Andy! I couldn't help it — and he knew how I'd suffered, too. He told you — to remember.

ANDREW: *(Stares at her for a moment, his rage ebbing away, an expression of deep pity gradually coming over his face. Then he glances down at his brother and speaks brokenly in a compassionate voice.)* Forgive me, Ruth — for his sake — and I'll remember — *(Ruth lets her hands fall from her face and looks at him uncomprehendingly. He lifts his eyes to hers and forces out falteringly.)* I — you — we've both made a mess of things! We must try to help each other — and — in time — we'll come to know what's right — *(Desperately.)* And perhaps we — *(But Ruth, if she is aware of his words, gives no sign. She remains silent, gazing at him dully with the sad humility of exhaustion, her mind already sinking back into that spent calm beyond the further troubling of any hope.)*

CURTAIN

from **"Anna Christie"** (1918)
from Act One

CHARACTERS

Anna
Larry
Marthy

[Anna Christopherson, a weary twenty-year-old prostitute who calls
herself "Anna Christie," arrives at "Jimmy-the-Priest's" saloon seeking
her father, a seaman she has not seen since childhood. Carrying a suit-
case, she appears at the entrance of the bar and slips into a seat. The
only other patron is Marthy, a much older woman. She observes
Anna's arrival, as she is approached by the bartender, Larry.]

ANNA: Gimme a whiskey — ginger ale on the side. *(Then, as Larry turns
to go, forcing a winning smile at him.)* And don't be stingy, baby.
LARRY: *(Sarcastically.)* Shall I serve it in a pail?
ANNA: *(With a hard laugh.)* That suits me down to the ground.
*(Larry goes into the bar. The two women size each other up with frank
stares. Larry comes back with the drink which he sets before Anna and returns to the bar again. Anna downs her drink at a gulp. Then, after a
moment, as the alcohol begins to rouse her, she turns to Marthy with a
friendly smile.)* Gee, I needed that bad, all right, all right!
MARTHY: *(Nodding her head sympathetically.)* Sure — yuh look all in.
Been on a bat?
ANNA: No — travelling — day and a half on a train. Had to sit up all
night in the dirty coach, too. Gawd, I thought I'd never get here!
MARTHY: *(With a start — looking at her intently.)* Where'd you come
from, huh?
ANNA: St. Paul — out in Minnesota.

MARTHY: *(Staring at her in amazement — slowly.)* So — yuh're — *(She suddenly bursts out into hoarse, ironical laughter.)* Gawd!

ANNA: All the way from Minnesota, sure. *(Flaring up.)* What are you laughing at? Me?

MARTHY: *(Hastily.)* No, honest, kid. I was thinkin' of somethin' else.

ANNA: *(Mollified — with a smile.)* Well, I wouldn't blame you, at that. Guess I do look rotten — yust out of the hospital two weeks. I'm going to have another 'ski. What d'you say? Have something on me?

MARTHY: Sure I will. T'anks. *(She calls.)* Hey, Larry! Little service! *(He comes in.)*

ANNA: Same for me.

MARTHY: Same here. *(Larry takes their glasses and goes out.)*

ANNA: Why don't you come sit over here, be sociable. I'm a dead stranger in this burg — and I ain't spoke a word with no one since day before yesterday.

MARTHY: Sure thing. *(She shuffles over to Anna's table and sits down opposite her. Larry brings the drinks and Anna pays him.)*

ANNA: Skoal! Here's how! *(She drinks.)*

MARTHY: Here's luck! *(She takes a gulp from her schooner.)*

ANNA: *(Taking a package of Sweet Caporal cigarettes from her bag.)* Let you smoke in here, won't they?

MARTHY: *(Doubtfully.)* Sure. *(Then with evident anxiety.)* Only trow it away if yuh hear someone comin'.

ANNA: *(Lighting one and taking a deep inhale.)* Gee, they're fussy in this dump, ain't they? *(She puffs, staring at the table top. Marthy looks her over with a new penetrating interest, taking in every detail of her face. Anna suddenly becomes conscious of this appraising stare — resentfully.)* Ain't nothing wrong with me, is there? You're look hard enough.

MARTHY: *(Irritated by the other's tone — scornfully.)* Ain't got to look much. I got your number the minute you stepped in the door.

ANNA: *(Her eyes narrowing.)* Ain't you smart! Well, I got your, too, without no trouble. You're me forty years from now. That's you! *(She gives a hard little laugh.)*

MARTHY: *(Angrily.)* Is that so? Well, I'll tell you straight, kiddo, that Marthy Owen never — *(She catches herself up short — with a grin.)* What are you and me scrappin' over? Let's cut it out, huh? Me, I don't want no hard feelin's with no one. *(Extending her hand.)* Shake and forget it, huh?

ANNA: *(Shakes her hand gladly.)* Only too glad to. I ain't looking for trouble. Let's have another. What d'you say?

MARTHY: *(Shaking her head.)* Not for mine. I'm full up. And you — Had anythin' to eat lately?

ANNA: Not since this morning on the train.

MARTHY: Then you better go easy on it, hadn't yuh?

ANNA: *(After a moment's hesitation.)* Guess you're right. I got to meet someone, too. But my nerves is on edge after that rotten trip.

MARTHY: Yuh said yuh was just outa the hospital?

ANNA: Two weeks ago? *(Leaning over to Marthy confidentially.)* The joint I was in out in St. Paul got raided. That was the start. The judge give all us girls thirty days. The others didn't seem to mind being in the cooler much. Some of 'em was used to it. But me, I couldn't stand it. It got my goat right — couldn't eat or sleep or nothing. I never could stand being caged up nowheres. I got good and sick and they had to send me to the hospital. It was nice there. I was sorry to leave it, honest!

MARTHY: *(After a slight pause.)* Did yuh say yuh got to meet someone here?

ANNA: Yes. Oh, not what you mean. It's my Old Man I got to meet. Honest! It's funny, too. I ain't seen him since I was a kid — don't even know what he looks like — yust had a letter every now and then. This was always the only address he give me to write him back. He's yanitor of some building here now — used to be a sailor.

MARTHY: *(Astonished.)* Janitor!

ANNA: Sure. And I was thinking, maybe, seeing he ain't never done a thing for me in my life, he might be willing to stake me to a room and eats till I get rested up. *(Wearily.)* Gee, I sure need that rest! I'm knocked out. *(The resignedly.)* But I ain't expecting much from him. Give you a kick when you're down, that's what all men do. *(With sudden passion.)* Men, I hate 'em — all of 'em! And I don't expect he'll turn out no better than the rest. *(Then with sudden interest.)* Say, do you hang out around this dump much?

MARTHY Oh, off and on.

ANNA: Then maybe you know him — my Old Man — or at least seen him?

MARTHY: It ain't old Chris, is it?

ANNA: Old Chris?

MARTHY: Chris Christopherson, his full name is.

ANNA: *(Excitedly.)* Yes, that's him! Anna Christopherson — that's my real name — only out there I called myself Anna Christie. So you know him, eh?

MARTHY: *(Evasively.)* Seen him about for years.

ANNA: Say, what's he like, tell me, honest?

MARTHY: Oh, he's short and —

ANNA: *(Impatiently.)* I don't care what he looks like. What kind is he?

MARTHY: *(Earnestly.)* Well, yuh can be your life, kid, he's as good an old guy as every walked on two feet. That goes!

ANNA: *(Pleased.)* I'm glad to hear it. Then you think he'll stake me to that rest cure I'm after?

MARTHY: *(Emphatically.)* Surest thing you know. *(Disgustedly.)* But where'd yuh get the idea he was a janitor?

ANNA: He wrote me he was himself.

MARTHY: Well, he was lyin'. He ain't. He's captain of a barge — five men under him.

ANNA: *(Disgusted in her turn.)* A barge? What kind of a barge?

MARTHY: Coal, mostly.

ANNA: A coal barge! *(With a harsh laugh.)* If that ain't a swell job to find your long lost Old Man working at! Gee, I knew something'd be bound to turn out wrong — always does with me. That puts my idea of his giving me a rest on the bum.

MARTHY: What d'yuh mean?

ANNA: I s'pose he lives on the boat, don't he?

MARTHY: Sure. What about it? Can't you live on it, too?

ANNA: *(Scornfully.)* Me? On a dirty coal barge! What d'you think I am?

MARTHY: *(Resentfully.)* What d'yuh know about barges, huh? Bet yuh ain't never seen one. That's what comes of his bringing yuh up inland — away from the old devil sea — where yuh'd be safe — Gawd!
(The irony of it strikes her sense of humor and she laughs hoarsely.)

ANNA: *(Angrily.)* His bringing me up! Is that what he tells people! I like his nerve! He let them cousins of my Old Woman's keep me on their farm and work me to death like a dog.

MARTHY: Well, he's got queer notions on some things. I've heard him say a farm was the best place for a kid.

ANNA: Sure. That's what he'd always answer back — and a lot of crazy stuff about staying away from the sea — stuff I couldn't make head or tail to. I thought he must be nutty.

MARTHY: He is on that one point. *(Casually.)* So yuh didn't fall for life on the farm, huh?

ANNA: I should say not! The old man of the family, his wife, and four sons — I had to slave for all of 'em. I was only a poor relation, and they treated me worse than they dare treat a hired girl. *(After a moment's hesitation — somberly.)* It was one of the sons — the youngest — started me — when I was sixteen. After that, I hate 'em so I'd killed 'em all if I'd stayed. So I run away — to St. Paul.

MARTHY: *(Who has been listening sympathetically.)* I've heard Old Chris talkin' about your bein' a nurse girl out there. Was that all a bluff yuh put up when yuh wrote him?

ANNA: Not on your life, it wasn't. It was true for two years. I didn't go wrong all at one jump. Being a nurse girl was yust what finished me. Taking care of other people's kids, always listening to their bawling and crying, caged in, when you're only a kid yourself and want to go out and see things. At last I got the chance — to get into that house. And you bet your life I took it! *(Defiantly.)* And I ain't sorry neither.

(After a pause — with bitter hatred.) It was all men's fault — the whole business. It was men on the farm ordering and beating me — and giving me the wrong start. Then when I was a nurse, it was men again hanging around, bothering me, trying to see what they could get. *(She gives a hard laugh.)* And now it's men all the time. Gawd, I hate 'em all, every mother's son of 'em. Don't you?

MARTHY: Oh, I dunno. There's good ones and bad ones, kid. You've just had a run of bad luck with 'em, that's all. Your Old Man, now — old Chris — he's a good one.

ANNA: *(Sceptically.)* He'll have to show me.

from **The Emperor Jones** (1920)
from Act One, Scene 1

CHARACTERS

Jones
Smithers

FROM SCENE 1

[Ex-Pullman train porter Brutus Jones has escaped to the West Indies
after murdering a man and declares himself emperor of a primitive
tribe of natives. He is stealing from the natives and plans to depart at
an appropriate moment. In an encounter with Smithers, an unscrupu-
lous white trader, he explains his plan for escape and reveals his disdain
for his "subjects."]

JONES: *(With indignant scorn.)* Look-a-heah, white man! Does you think
I'se a natural bo'n fool? Give me credit fo' havih' some sense, fo'
Lawd's sake! Don't you s'pose I'se looked ahead and made sho' of all
de chances? I'se gone out in dat big forest, pretendin' to hunt, so
many times dat I knows it high an' low like a book. I could go
through on dem trails wid my eyes shut. *(With great contempt.)*
Think dese ig'nerent bush niggers dat ain't got brains enuff to know
deir own names even can catch Brutus Jones? Huh, I s'pects not!
Not on yo' life! why, man, de white men went after me wid blood-
hounds where I come from an' I jes' laughs at 'em. It's a shame to
fool dese black trash around heah, dey're so easy. You watch me,
man'. I'll make dem look sick, I will. I'll be 'cross de plain to de edge
of de forest by time dark comes. Once in de woods in de night, dey
got a swell chance o' findin' dis baby! Dawn tomorrow I'll be out at
de oder side and on de coast whar dat French gunboat is stayin'. She
picks me up, take me to the Martinique when she go dar, and dere

I is safe wid a mighty big bankroll in my jeans. It's easy as rollin' off a log.

SMITHERS: *(Maliciously.)* But s'posin' somethin' 'appens wrong an' they do nab yer?

JONES: *(Decisively.)* Dey don't — dat's de answer.

SMITHERS: But, just for argyment's sake — what'd you do?

JONES: *(Frowning.)* I'se got five lead bullets in dis gun good enuff fo' common bush niggers — and after dat I got de silver bullet left to cheat 'em out o' gittin' me.

SMITHERS: *(Jeeringly.)* Ho, I was fergettin' that silver bullet. You'll bump yourself orf in style, won't yer? Blimey!

JONES: *(Gloomily.)* You kin bet yo' whole roll on one thing, white man. Dis baby plays out his string to de end and when he quits, he quits wid a bang de way he ought. Silver bullet ain't none too good for him when he go, dat's a fac' I — *(Then shaking off his nervousness — with a confident laugh.)* Sho'! what is I talkin' about? Ain't come to dat yit and I never will — not wid trash niggers like dese yere. *(Boastfully.)* Silver bullet bring me luck anyway. I kin outguess, outrun, outfight, an' outplay de whole lot o' dem all ovah de board any time o' de day er night! You watch me! *(From the distant hills comes the faint, steady thump of a tom-tom, low and vibrating. It starts at a rate exactly corresponding to normal pulse beat — 72 to the minute — and continues at a gradually accelerated rate from this point uninterruptedly to the very end of the play. Jones starts at the sound. A strange look of apprehension creeps into his face for a moment as he listens. Then he asks, with an attempt to regain his most casual manner.)* What's dat drum beatin' fo'?

from **The Emperor Jones** (1920)
from Act One, Scene 3

CHARACTERS

Jones

FROM SCENE 3

[As Jones makes his escape into the jungle, he is overtaken by his fears. As the ominous thump of the tom-tom continues in the distance, he talks to himself.]

JONES: De moon's rizen. Does you heah dat, nigger? You gits more light from dis out. No mo' buttin' yo' fool head agin' de trunks an' scratchin' de hide off yo' legs in de bushes. Now you sees whar yo'se gwine. So cheer up! From now on you has a snap. *(He steps just to the rear of the triangular clearing and mops off his face on his sleeve. He has lost his Panama hat. His face is scratched, his brilliant uniform shows several large rents.)* what time's it gittin' to be, I wonder? I dassent light no match to find out. Phoo'. It's wa'm an' dats a fac'! *(Wearily.)* How long r been makin' tracks in dese woods? Must be hours an' hours. Seems like fo'evah! Yit can't be, when de moon's jes' riz. Dis am a long night fo' yo', yo' Majesty! *(With a mournful chuckle.)* Majesty! Der ain't much majesty 'bout dis baby now. *(With attempted cheerfulness.)* Never min'. It's all part o' de game. Dis night come to an end like everything else. And when you gits dar safe and has dat bankroll in yo' hands you laughs at all dis. *(He starts to whistle but checks himself abruptly.)* What yo' whistlin' for, you po' dope! Want all de won' to heah you? *(He stops talking to listen.)* Heah dat ole drum! Sho' gits nearer from de sound. Dey're packin' it along wid 'em. Time fo' me to move. *(He takes a step forward, then stops — worriedly.)* What's dat odder queer clicketty sound I heah? Den it is! Sound close! Sound like — sound like — Fo' God sake, sound like some nigger was shootin' crap! *(Frightenedly.)* I better beat it quick when I gits dem notions. *(He walks quickly into the clear space — then stands transfixed as he sees Jeff in a terrified gasp.)* Who dar? Who dat? Is dat you, Jeff? *(Starting toward the other, forgetful for a moment of his surroundings and really believing it is a living man that he sees — in a tone of happy relief.)* Jeff! I'se sho' mighty glad to see you! Dey tol' me you done died from dat razor cut I gives you. *(Stopping suddenly, bewilderedly.)* But how you come to be heah, nigger? *(He stares fascinatedly at the other who continues his mechanical play with the dice. Jones' eyes begin to roll wildly. He stutters.)* Ain't you gwine — look up — can't you speak to me? Is you — is you — a ha'nt? *(He jerks out his revolver in a frenzy of terrified rage.)* Nigger, I kills you dead once. Has I got to kill you agin? You take it den. *(He fires. When the smoke clears away Jeff has disappeared. Jones stands trembling — then with a certain reassurance.)* He's gone, anyway. Ha'nt or no ha'nt, dat shot fix him. *(The beat of the far-off tom-tom is perceptibly louder and more rapid. Jones becomes conscious of it — with a start, looking back over his shoulder.)* Dey's gittin' near! Dey'se comin' fast! And heah I is shootin' shots to let 'em know jes' whar I is. Oh, Gorry, I'se got to run. *(Forgetting the path he plunges wildly into the underbrush in the rear and disappears in the shadow.)*

[As the play continues to its conclusion, Jones eventually succumbs to his fears, the vengeance of the natives, and a silver bullet.]

from **The Hairy Ape** (1921)
from Scene 2

CHARACTERS

> Mildred Douglas
> Aunt
> Second Engineer

[Subtitled "A Comedy of Ancient and Modern Life," *The Hairy Ape*
limited its "comedy" to an ironic absurdity evident in its examination
of the alienation of the individual in a technological, capitalist society,
much of which is expressed in the play via expressionistic techniques,
as in O'Neill's *The Emperor Jones*. The play focuses on Yank Smith, a
brutish, inarticulate stoker on a passenger liner. He has lived his life in
unquestioned service to the demands of his job until he encounters
Mildred Douglas, the pampered daughter of the ship line's president.
The meeting sets Yank's tragedy in motion. O'Neill's evocative stage
descriptions, typical of his plays, set the scene and introduce Mildred,
who is traveling on the liner with her aunt.]

> *Two days out. A section of the promenade deck. Mildred Douglas and her
> aunt are discovered reclining in deck chairs. The former is a girl of twenty,
> slender, delicate, with a pale, pretty face marred by a self-conscious expres-
> sion of disdainful superiority. She looks fretful, nervous and discontented,
> bored by her own anemia. Her aunt is a pompous and proud — and fat —
> old lady. She is a type even to the point of a double chin and lorgnettes.
> She is dressed pretentiously, as if afraid her face alone would never indi-
> cate her position in life. Mildred is dressed all in white.*
>
> *The impression to be conveyed by this scene is one of the beautiful, vivid
> life of the sea all about — sunshine on the deck in a great flood, the fresh
> sea wind blowing across it. In the midst of this, these two incongruous, ar-
> tificial figures, inert and disharmonious, the elder like a gray lump of*

dough touched up with rouge, the younger looking as if the vitality of her stock had been sapped before she was conceived, so that she is the expression not of its life energy but merely of the artificialities that energy had won for itself in the spending.

MILDRED: *(Looking up with affected dreaminess.)* How the black smoke swirls back against the sky! Is it not beautiful?

AUNT: *(Without looking up.)* I dislike smoke of any kind.

MILDRED: My great-grandmother smoked a pipe — a clay pipe.

AUNT: *(Ruffling.)* Vulgar!

MILDRED: She was too distant a relative to be vulgar. Time mellows pipes.

AUNT: *(Pretending boredom but irritated.)* Did the sociology you took up at college teach you that — to play the ghoul on every possible occasion, excavating old bones? Why not let your great-grandmother rest in her grave?

MILDRED: *(Dreamily.)* With her pipe beside her — puffing in Paradise.

AUNT: *(With spite.)* Yes, you are a natural born ghoul. You are even getting to look like one, my dear.

MILDRED: *(In a passionless tone.)* I detest you, Aunt. *(Looking at her critically.)* Do you know what you remind me of? Of a cold pork pudding against a background of linoleum tablecloth in the kitchen of a — but the possibilities are wearisome. *(She closes her eyes.)*

AUNT: *(With a bitter laugh.)* Merci for your candor. But since I am and must be your chaperon — in appearance, at least — let us patch up some sort of armed truce. For my part you are quite free to indulge any pose of eccentricity that beguiles you — as long as you observe the amenities —

MILDRED: *(Drawling.)* The inanities?

AUNT: *(Going on as if she hadn't heard.)* After exhausting the morbid thrills of social service work on New York's East Side — how they must have hated you, by the way, the poor that you made so much poorer in their own eyes! — you are now bent on making your slumming international. Well, I hope Whitechapel will provide the needed nerve tonic. Do not ask me to chaperon you there, however. I told your father I would not. I loathe deformity. We will hire an army of detectives and you may investigate everything — they allow you to see.

MILDRED: *(Protesting with a trace of genuine earnestness.)* Please do not mock at my attempts to discover how the other half lives. Give me credit for some sort of groping sincerity in that at least. I would like to help them. I would like to be some use in the world. Is it my fault I don't know how? I would like to be sincere, to touch life some-where. *(With a weary bitterness.)* But I'm afraid I have neither the vitality nor integrity. All that was burnt out in our stock before I was born. Grandfather's blast furnaces, flaming to the sky, melting steel, making millions — then father keeping those home fires burn-ing, making more millions — and little me at the tail-end of it all. I'm a waste product in the Bessemer process — like the millions. Or rather, I inherit the acquired trait of the by-product, wealth, but none of the energy, none of the strength of the steel that made it. I am sired by gold and damned by it, as they say at the race track — damned in more ways than one. *(She laughs mirthlessly.)*

AUNT: *(Unimpressed — superciliously.)* You seem to be going in for sin-cerity today. It isn't becoming to you, really — except as an obvious pose. Be as artificial as you are, I advise. There's a sort of sincerity in that, you know. And, after all, you must confess you like that better.

MILDRED: *(Again affected and bored.)* Yes, I suppose I do. Pardon me for my outburst. When a leopard complains of its spots, it must sound rather grotesque. *(In a mocking tone.)* Purr, little leopard. Purr, scratch, tear, kill, gorge yourself and be happy — only stay in the jungle where your spots are camouflage. In a cage they make you conspicuous.

AUNT: I don't know what you are talking about.

MILDRED: It would be rude to talk about anything to you. Let's just talk. *(She looks at her wrist watch.)* Well, thank goodness, it's about time for them to come for me. That ought to give me a new thrill, Aunt.

AUNT: *(Affectedly troubled.)* You don't mean to say you're really going? The dirt — the heat must be frightful —

MILDRED: Grandfather started as a puddler. I should have inherited an immunity to the heat that would make a salamander shiver. It will be fun to put it to the test.

AUNT: But don't you have to have the captain's — or someone's — permission to visit the stokehole?

MILDRED: *(With a triumphant smile.)* I have it — both his and the chief engineer's. Oh, they didn't want to at first, in spite of my social service credentials. They didn't seem a bit anxious that I should investigate how the other half lives and works on a ship. So I had to tell them that my father, the president of Nazareth Steel, chairman of the board of directors of this line, had told me it would be all right.

AUNT: He didn't.

MILDRED: How naïve age makes one! But I said he did, Aunt. I even said he had given me a letter to them — which I had lost. And they were afraid to take the chance that I might be lying. *(Excitedly.)* So it's ho! for the stokehole. The second engineer is to escort me. *(Looking at her watch again.)* It's time. And here he comes, I think. *(The Second Engineer enters. He is a husky, fine-looking man of thirty-five or so. He stops before the two and tips his cap, visibly embarrassed and ill-at-ease.)*

SECOND ENGINEER: Miss Douglas?

MILDRED: Yes. *(Throwing off her rugs and getting to her feet.)* Are we all ready to start?

SECOND ENGINEER: In just a second, ma'am. I'm waiting for the Fourth. He's coming along.

MILDRED: *(With a scornful smile.)* You don't care to shoulder this responsibility alone, is that it?

SECOND ENGINEER: *(Forcing a smile.)* Two are better than one. *(Disturbed by her eyes, glances out to sea — blurts out.)* A fine day we're having.

MILDRED: Is it?

SECOND ENGINEER: A nice warm breeze —

MILDRED: It feels cold to me.

SECOND ENGINEER: But it's hot enough in the sun —

MILDRED: Not hot enough for me. I don't like Nature. I was never athletic.

SECOND ENGINEER: *(Forcing a smile.)* Well, you'll find it hot enough where you're going.

MILDRED: Do you mean hell?

SECOND ENGINEER: *(Flabbergasted, decides to laugh.)* Ho-ho! No, I mean the stokehole.

MILDRED: My grandfather was a puddler. He played with boiling steel.

SECOND ENGINEER: *(All at sea — uneasily.)* Is that so? Hum, you'll excuse me, ma'am, but are you intending to wear that dress?

MILDRED: Why not?

SECOND ENGINEER: You'll likely rub against oil and dirt. It can't be helped.

MILDRED: It doesn't matter. I have lots of white dresses.

SECOND ENGINEER: I have an old coat you might throw over —

MILDRED: I have fifty dresses like this. I will throw this one into the sea when I come back. That ought to wash it clean, don't you think?

SECOND ENGINEER: There's ladders to climb down that are none too clean — and dark alleyways —

MILDRED: I will wear this very dress and none other.

SECOND ENGINEER: No offense meant. It's none of my business. I was only warning you —

MILDRED: Warning? That sounds thrilling.

SECOND ENGINEER: *(Looking down the deck — with a sigh of relief.)* There's the Fourth now. He's waiting for us. If you'll come —

MILDRED: Go on. I'll follow you. *(He goes. Mildred turns a mocking smile on her aunt.)* An oaf — but a handsome, virile oaf.

AUNT: *(Scornfully.)* Poser!

MILDRED: Take care. He said there were dark alleyways —

AUNT: *(In the same tone.)* Poser!

MILDRED: *(Biting her lips angrily.)* You are right. But would that my millions were not so anemically chaste!

AUNT: Yes, for a fresh pose I have no doubt you would drag the name of Douglas in the gutter!

MILDRED: From which it sprang. Good-bye, Aunt. Don't pray too hard that I may fall into the fiery furnace.

AUNT: Poser!

MILDRED: *(Viciously.)* Old hag! *(She slaps her aunt insultingly across the face and walks off, laughing gaily.)*

AUNT: *(Screams after her.)* I said poser!

from **The Hairy Ape** (1921)
from Scene 3

CHARACTERS

Paddy
Yank

[Scene 3 finds Yank and the other stokers laboring deep in the bowels of the ship.]

The men shovel with a rhythmic motion, swinging as on a pivot from the coal which lies in heaps on the floor behind to hurl it into the flaming mouths before them. There is a tumult of noise — the brazen clang of the furnace doors as they are flung open or slammed shut, the grating, teeth-gritting grind of steel against steel, of crunching coal. This clash of sounds stuns one's ears with its rending dissonance. But there is order in it, rhythm, a mechanical regulated recurrence, a tempo. And rising above all, making the air hum with the quiver of liberated energy, the roar of leaping flames in the furnaces, the monotonous throbbing beat of the engines.

As the curtain rises, the furnace doors are shut. The men are taking a breathing spell. One or two are arranging the coal behind them, pulling it into more accessible heaps. The others can be dimly made out leaning on their shovels in relaxed attitudes of exhaustion.

PADDY: *(From somewhere in the line — plaintively.)* Yerra, will this divil's own watch nivir end? Me back is broke. I'm destroyed entirely.

YANK: *(From the center of the line — with exuberant scorn.)* Aw, yuh make me sick! Lie down and croak, why don't yuh? Always beefin', dat's you! Say, dis is a cinch! Dis was made for me! It's my meat, get me! *(A whistle is blown — a thin, shrill note from somewhere overhead in the darkness. Yank curses without resentment.)* Dere's de damn engineer crackin' de whip. He tinks we're loafin'.

PADDY: *(Vindictively.)* God stiffen him!

YANK: (*In an exultant tone of command.*) Come on, youse guys! Git into de game! She's gittin' hungry! Pile some grub in her. Trow it into her belly! Come on now, all of youse! Open her up! (*At this last all the men, who have followed his movements of getting into position, throw open their furnace doors with a deafening clang. The fiery light floods over their shoulder as they bend round for the coal. Rivulets of sooty sweat have traced maps on their backs. The enlarged muscles form bunches of high light and shadow.*)

YANK: (*Chanting a count as he shovels without seeming effort.*) One — two — tree — (*His voice rising exultantly in the joy of battle.*) Dat's de stuff! Let her have it! All togedder now! Sling it into her! Let her ride! Shoot de piece now! Call de toin on her! Drive her into it! Feel her move! Watch her smoke! Speed, dat's her middle name! Give her coal, youse guys! Coal, dat's her booze! Drink it up, baby! Let's see yuh sprint! Dig in and gain a lap! Dere she go-o-es. (*This last in the chanting formula of the gallery gods at the six-day bike race. He slams his furnace door shut. The others do likewise with as much unison as their wearied bodies will permit. The effect is of one fiery eye after another being blotted out with a series of accompanying bangs.*)

PADDY: (*Groaning.*) Me back is broke. I'm bate out — bate — (*There is a pause. Then the inexorable whistle sounds again from the dim regions above the electric light. There is a growl of cursing rage from all sides.*)

YANK: (*Shaking his fist upward — contemptuously.*) Take it easy dere, you! Who d'yuh tink's runnin' dis game, me or you? When I git ready, we move. Not before! When I git ready, get me!

VOICES: (*Approvingly.*) That's the stuff!
Yank tal him, py golly!
Yank ain't affeered.
Goot poy, Yank!
Give him hell!
Tell 'im 'e's a bloody swine!
Bloody slave-driver!

YANK: (*Contemptuously.*) He ain't got no noive. He's yellow, get me? All de engineers is yellow. Dey got streaks a mile wide. Aw, to hell wit' him! Let's move, youse guys. We had a rest. Come on, she needs it! Give her pep! It ain't for him. Him and his whistle, dey don't belong. But we belong, see! We gotter feed de baby! Come on! *(He turns and flings his furnace door open. They all follow his lead. At this instant the Second and Fourth Engineers enter from the darkness on the left with Mildred between them. She starts, turns paler, her pose is crumbling, she shivers with fright in spite of the blazing heat, but forces herself to leave the Engineers and take a few steps nearer the men. She is right behind Yank. All this happens quickly while the men have their backs turned.)*

YANK: Come on, youse guys! *(He is turning to get coal when the whistle sounds again in a peremptory, irritating note. This drives Yank into a sudden fury. While the other men have turned full around and stopped dumfounded by the spectacle of Mildred standing there in her white dress, Yank does not turn far enough to see her. Besides, his head is thrown back, he blinks upward through the murk trying to find the owner of the whistle, he brandishes his shovel murderously over his head in one hand, pounding on his chest, gorilla-like with the other, shouting.)* Toin off dat whistle! Come down outa dere, yuh yellow, brass-buttoned, Belfast bum, yuh! Come down and I'll knock yer brains out! Yuh lousy, stinkin', yellow mutt of a Catholic-moiderin' bastard! Come down and I'll moider yuh! Pullin' dat whistle on me, huh? I'll show yuh! I'll crash yer skull in! I'll drive yer teet' down yer troat! I'll slam yer nose trou de back of yer head! I'll cut yer guts out for a nickel, yuh lousy boob, yuh dirty, crummy, muck-eatin' son of a — *(Suddenly he becomes conscious of all the other men staring at something directly behind his back. He whirls defensively with a snarling, murderous growl, crouching to spring, his lips drawn back over his teeth, his small eyes gleaming ferociously. He sees Mildred, like a white apparition in the full light from the open furnace doors. He glares into her eyes, turned to stone. As for her, during his speech she had listened, paralyzed with horror, terror, her whole personality crushed, beaten in, collapsed, by the terrific impact of this unknown, abysmal brutality, naked and shameless. As she looks at his gorilla face, as his eyes bore into hers, she utters a low, choking cry and shrinks away from him, putting both hands up before her eyes to shut out the sight of his face, to protect her own. This startles Yank to a reaction. His mouth falls open, his eyes grow bewildered.)*

MILDRED: *(About to faint — to the Engineers, who now have her one by each arm — whimperingly.)* Take me away! Oh, the filthy beast! *(She faints. They carry her quickly back, disappearing in the darkness at the left, rear. An iron door clangs shut. Rage and bewildered fury rush back into Yank. He feels himself insulted in some unknown fashion in the very heart of his pride.)*

YANK: *(He roars.)* God damn yuh! *(And hurls his shovel after them at the door, which has just closed. It hits the steel bulkhead with a clang and falls clattering on the steel floor. From overhead the whistle sounds again in a long, angry, insistent command.)*

from **The Hairy Ape** (1921)
from Scene 8

CHARACTERS

Yank

[Mildred's reaction sparks a soul-searching journey for Yank, including a visit to New York City's Fifth Avenue where his inappropriate behavior lands him in jail. He discovers there is no place for him there either when he is denied membership in the "Wobblies," a leftist prison gang, despite his offer to blow up the Douglas Steel Works for them. Released from prison, the despairing, uncomprehending Yank visits a gorilla at the zoo and feels a connection with the caged beast.]

> *Twilight of the next day. The monkey house at the Zoo. One spot of clear gray light falls on the front of one cage so that the interior can be seen. The other cages are vague, shrouded in shadow from which chatterings pitched in a conversational tone can be heard. On the one cage a sign from which the word "gorilla" stands out. The gigantic animal himself is seen squatting on his haunches on a bench in much the same attitude as Rodin's "Thinker." Yank enters from the left. Immediately a chorus of angry chattering and screeching breaks out. The gorilla turns his eyes but makes no sound or move.*

YANK: *(With a hard, bitter laugh.)* Welcome to your city, huh? Hail, hail, de gang's all here! *(At the sound of his voice the chattering dies away into an attentive silence. Yank walks up to the gorilla's cage and, leaning over the railing, stares in at its occupant, who stares back at him, silent and motionless. There is a pause of dead stillness. Then Yank begins to talk in a friendly confidential tone, half-mockingly, but with a deep undercurrent of sympathy.)* Say, yuh're some hard-lookin' guy, ain't yuh? I seen lots of tough nuts dat de gang called gorillas, but yuh're de foist real one I ever seen. Some chest yuh got, and shoulders, and dem arms and mits! I bet yuh got a punch in eider fist dat'd knock 'em all silly! *(This with genuine admiration. The gorilla, as if he understood, stands upright, swelling out his chest and pounding it with his fist. Yank grins sympathetically.)* Sure, I get yuh. Yuh challenge de whole woild, huh? Yuh got what I was sayin' even if yuh muffled de woids. *(Then bitterness creeping in.)* And why wouldn't yuh get me? Ain't we both members of de same club — de Hairy Apes? *(They stare at each other — a pause — then Yank goes on slowly and bitterly.)* So yuh're what she seen when she looked at me, de white-faced tart! I was you to her, get me? On'y outa de cage — broke out — free to moider her, see? Sure! Dat's what she tought. She wasn't wise dat I was in a cage, too — worser'n yours — sure — a damn sight — 'cause you got some chanct to bust loose — but me — *(He grows confused.)* Aw, hell! It's all wrong, ain't it? *(A pause.)* I s'pose yuh wanter know what I'm doin' here, huh? I been warmin' a bench down to de Battery — ever since last night. Sure. I seen de sun come up. Dat was pretty, too — all red and pink and green. I was lookin' at de skyscrapers — steel — and all de ships comin' in, sailin' out, all over de oith — and dey was steel, too. De sun was warm, dey wasn't no clouds, and dere was a breeze blowin'. Sure, it was great stuff. I got it aw right — what Paddy said about dat bein' de right dope — on'y I couldn't get in it, see? I couldn't belong in dat. It was over my head. And I kept tinkin' — and den I beat it up here to see what youse was like. And I waited till dey was all gone to git yuh alone. Say, how d'yuh feel sittin' in dat pen all de time, havin' to stand for 'em comin' and starin' at yuh — de white-faced, skinny tarts and de boobs what marry 'em — makin' fun of yuh, laughin' at yuh, gittin' scared of yuh — damn 'em! *(He pounds on the rail with his fist. The gorilla rattles the bars of his cage and snarls. All the other monkeys set up an angry chattering in the darkness. Yank goes on excitedly.)* Sure! Dat's de way it hits me, too. On'y yuh're lucky, see? Yuh don't belong wit' 'em and yuh know it. But me, I belong wit' 'em — but I don't, see? Dey don't belong wit' me, dat's what. Get me? Tinkin' is hard — *(He passes one hand across his forehead with a painful gesture. The gorilla growls impatiently. Yank goes on gropingly.)* It's dis way, what I'm drivin' at. Youse can sit and dope dream in de past, green woods, de jungle and de rest of it. Den yuh belong and dey don't. Den yuh kin laugh at 'em, see? Yuh're de champ of de woild. But me — I ain't got no past to tink in, nor nothin' dats comin', on'y what's now — and dat don't belong. Sure, yuh're de best off! Yuh can't tink, can yuh? Yuh can't talk neider. But I kin make a bluff at talkin' and tinkin' — a'most git away wit' it — a'most! — and dat's where de joker comes in. *(He laughs.)* I ain't on oith and I ain't in heaven, get me? I'm in de middle tryin' to separate 'em, takin' all de woist punches from bot' of 'em. Maybe dat's what dey call hell, huh? But you, yuh're at de bottom. You belong! Sure! Yuh're de on'y one in de woild dat does, yuh lucky stiff! *(The gorilla growls proudly.)* And dat's why dey gotter put yuh in a cage, see? *(The gorilla roars angrily.)* Sure! Yuh get me. It beats it when yuh try to tink it or talk it — it's way down — deep — behind — you 'n' me we feel it. Sure! Bot' members of dis club! *(He laughs — then in a savage tone.)* What de hell! T' hell wit' it! A little action, dat's our meat! Dat belongs! Knock 'em down and keep bustin' 'em till dey croaks yuh wit' a gat — wit' steel! Sure! Are yuh game? Dey've looked at youse, ain't dey — in a cage? Wanter git even? Wanter wind up like a sport 'stead of croakin' slow in dere? *(The gorilla roars an emphatic affirmative. Yank goes on with a sort of furious exaltation.)* Sure! Yuh're reg'lar! Yuh'll stick to de finish! Me 'n' you, huh? — bot' members of this club! We'll put up one last star bout dat'll knock 'em offen deir seats! Dey'll have to make de cages stronger after we're trou! *(The gorilla is straining at his bars, growling, hopping from one foot to the other. Yank takes a jimmy from under his coat and forces the lock on the cage door. He throws this open.)* Pardon from de governor! Step out and shake hands. I'll take yuh for a walk down Fif' Avenoo. We'll knock 'em offen de oith and croak wit' de band playin'. Come on, Brother. *(The gorilla scrambles gingerly out of his cage. Goes to Yank and stands looking at him. Yank keeps his mocking tone — holds out his hand.)* Shake   de secret grip of our order. *(Something, the tone of mockery, perhaps, suddenly enrages the animal. With a spring, he wraps his huge arms around Yank in a murderous hug. There is a crackling snap of crushed ribs — a gasping cry, still mocking, from Yank.)* Hey, I didn't say kiss me! *(The gorilla lets the crushed body slip to the floor; stands over it uncertainly, considering; then picks it up, throws it in the cage, shuts the door, and shuffles off menacingly into the darkness at left. A great uproar of frightened chattering and whimpering comes from the other cages. Then Yank moves, groaning, opening his eyes, and there is silence. He mutters painfully.)* Say — dey oughter match him — wit' Zybszko. He got me, aw right. I'm trou. Even him didn't tink I belonged. *(Then, with sudden passionate despair.)* Christ, where do I get off at? Where do I fit in? *(Checking himself as suddenly.)* Aw, what de hell! No squawkin', see! No quittin', get me! Croak wit' your boots on! *(He grabs hold of the bars of the cage and hauls himself painfully to his feet — looks around him bewilderedly — forces a mocking laugh.)* In de cage, huh? *(In the strident tones of a circus barker.)* Ladies and gents, step forward and take a slant at de one and only — *(His voice weakening.)* — one and original — Hairy ape from de wilds of — *(He slips in a heap on the floor and dies. The monkeys set up a chattering, whimpering wail. And, perhaps, the Hairy Ape at last belongs.)*

CURTAIN

THE READING ROOM

YOUNG ACTORS AND THEIR TEACHERS

Alexander, Doris. *Eugene O'Neill's Creative Struggle: The Decisive Decade, 1924–33.* University Park, Penn.: Penn State University Press, 1992.

Berlin, Normand. *Eugene O'Neill.* New York: Grove Press, Inc., 1982.

Black, Stephen A. "Ella O'Neill's Addiction," *The Eugene O'Neill Newsletter* IX.1 (Spring 1985): 24–26.

_____. *Eugene O'Neill: Beyond Mourning and Tragedy.* New Haven, Conn.: Yale University Press, 1999.

Bloom, Stephen F. *Student Companion to Eugene O'Neill.* Westport, Conn.: Greenwood, 2007.

Boulton, Agnes. *Part of a Long Story: Eugene O'Neill as a Young Man in Love.* Garden City, N.Y.: Doubleday, 1958.

Clark, Barrett H. *Eugene O'Neill: The Man and His Plays.* New York: Robert M. McBride, 1929.

Falk, Doris V. *Eugene O'Neill's Last Plays: Separating Art from Autobiography.* Athens: University of Georgia, 2005.

Frenz, Horst. *Eugene O'Neill.* New York: Frederick Ungar, 1971.

Gelb, Arthur, and Barbara Gelb. *O'Neill.* New York: Harper and Row, 1962.

_____. *O'Neill: Life with Monte Cristo.* New York: Applause, 2000.

Hermann, Spring. *A Student's Guide to Eugene O'Neill.* New York: Enslow Publishers, 2009.

Ranald, Margaret Loftus. *The Eugene O'Neill Companion.* Westport, Conn.: Greenwood Press, 1984.

This extensive bibliography lists books about the playwright according to whom the books might be of interest. If you would like to research further something that interests you in the text, lists of references, sources cited, and editions used in this book are found in this section.

SCHOLARS, STUDENTS, PROFESSORS

Ahuja, Chapman. *Tragedy, Modern Temper, and O'Neill*. Atlantic High-
lands, N.J.: Humanities Press, 1983.

Bogard, Travis. *The Theatre We Worked For: The Letters of Eugene
O'Neill and Kenneth Macgowan*. New Haven, Conn.: Yale University
Press, 1982.

_____. *The Unknown O'Neill: Unpublished or Unfamiliar Writings
of Eugene O'Neill*. New Haven and London: Yale University Press,
1988.

_____. *Eugene O'Neill at Tao House*. Contra Costra, Calif.: West-
ern National Parks Association, 1989.

Bryer, Jackson R., ed. *Eugene O'Neill: The Contemporary Reviews*. New
York: Cambridge University Press, 2009.

Commins, Dorothy, ed. *Love and Admiration and Respect: The
O'Neill–Commins Correspondence*. Durham, N.C.: Duke University
Press, 1986.

Dowling, Robert. *Critical Companion to Eugene O'Neill*. New York: Facts
on File, 2009.

Dubost, Thierry. *Struggle, Defeat, or Rebirth: Eugene O'Neill's Vision of
Humanity*. Jefferson, N.C.: McFarland and Company, 1996.

Falk, Doris V. *The Tempering of Eugene O'Neill*. New York: Harcourt,
Brace & World, 1962.

Fleche, Anne. *Mimetic Disillusion: Eugene O'Neill, Tennessee Williams,
and U.S. Dramatic Realism*. Tuscaloosa: University of Alabama Press,
1997.

Houchin, John H., ed. *The Critical Response to Eugene O'Neill*. Westport,
Conn.: Greenwood Press, 1993.

Liu, Haiping, and Lowell Swortzell, ed. *Eugene O'Neill in China: An International Centerary Celebration*. Westport, Conn.: Greenwood Press,
1992.

Manheim, Michael, ed. *The Cambridge Companion to Eugene O'Neill*.
Cambridge: Cambridge University Press, 1998.

_____. *Eugene O'Neill's New Language of Kinship*. Syracuse,
N.Y.: Syracuse University Press, 1982.

Martine, James J., ed. *Critical Essays on Eugene O'Neill*. Boston: G. K.
Hall, 1984.

Maufort, Marc. *Songs of American Experience. The Vision of O'Neill and Melville.* New York: Peter Lang, 1990.

Miliora, Maria T. *Narcissism, the Family and Madness: A Self-Psychological Study of Eugene O'Neill and His Plays.* New York: Peter Lang, 2000.

Moorton, Richard F., Jr. ed. *Eugene O'Neill's Century: Centennial Views on America's Foremost Tragic Dramatist.* Westport, Conn.: Greenwood Press, 1991.

Pfister, Joel. *Staging Depth: Eugene O'Neill and the Politics of Psychological Discourse.* Chapel Hill: University of North Carolina Press, 1995.

Porter, Laurin. *The Banished Prince: Time, Memory, and Ritual in the Late Plays of Eugene O'Neill.* Ann Arbor, Mich.: UMI Research Press, 1988.

Robinson, James A. *Eugene O'Neill and Oriental Thought.* Carbondale: Southern Illinois University Press, 1982.

Sanborn, Ralph, and Barrett H. Clark. *A Bibliography of the Works of Eugene O'Neill.* New York: Random House, 1931.

Shaughnessy, Edward L. "Ella O'Neill and the Imprint of Faith," *The Eugene O'Neill Review* 16.2 (Fall 1992): 29–43.

Siebold, Thomas, ed. *Readings on Eugene O'Neill.* New York: Greenhaven Press, 1998.

Skinner, Richard Dana. *Eugene O'Neill. A Poet's Quest.* New York and Toronto: Longmans, Green & Co., 1935.

Smith, Madeline C., and Richard Eaton. *Eugene O'Neill: An Annotated International Bibliography, 1973–1999.* Jefferson, N.C.: McFarland, 2001.

Stroupe, John, ed. *Critical Approaches to O'Neill.* New York: AMS Press, 1988.

Wainscott, Ronald H., "Exploring the Religion of the Dead: Philip Moeller Directs O'Neill's *Mourning Becomes Electra*," *Theatre History Studies* 7 (1987): 28–39.

_____. *Staging O'Neill: The Experimental Years.* New Haven, Conn.: Yale University Press, 1988.

THEATERS, PRODUCERS

Black, Stephen A., "O'Neill and the Old Ham," *The Eugene O'Neill Review* 17.1–2 (Spring–Fall 1993): 77–81.

Bogard, Travis, and Jackson R. Bryer, eds. *Selected Letters of Eugene O'Neill*. New York: Limelight Editions, 1994.

Diggins, John Patrick. *Eugene O'Neill's America: Desire Under Democracy*. Chicago, Ill.: University of Chicago, 2007.

Engel, Edwin. *The Haunted Heroes of Eugene O'Neill*. Cambridge, Mass.: Harvard University Press, 1953.

Estrin, Mark W. *Conversations with Eugene O'Neill*. Jackson: University Press of Mississippi, 1990.

King, William Davies, ed. *The Correspondence of Agnes Boulton and Eugene O'Neill*. Rutherford, N.J.: Fairleigh Dickinson University Press, 2000.

Orlandello, John. *O'Neill on Film*. Rutherford, N.J.: Fairleigh Dickinson University Press, 1982.

Roberts, Arthur W., and Nancy. *As Ever, Gene: The Letters of Eugene O'Neill to George Jean Nathan*. Rutherford, N.J.: Fairleigh Dickinson University, 1987.

Shaughnessy, Edward L. *Eugene O'Neill in Ireland: The Critical Reception*. Westport, Conn.: Greenwood, 1988.

ACTORS, DIRECTORS, PROFESSIONALS

Atkinson, Jennifer McCabe, ed. *Children of the Sea and Three Other Unpublished Plays by Eugene O'Neill*. Washington, D.C.: NCR Microcard Editions, 1972.

Barlow, Judith E. *Final Acts. The Creation of Three Late O'Neill Plays*. Athens: University of Georgia Press, 1984.

Bogard, Travis. *Contour in Time: The Plays of Eugene O'Neill*. New York: Oxford University Press, 1988.

Bowen, Croswell, and Shane O'Neill. *The Curse of the Misbegotten: A Tale of the House of O'Neill*. New York: McGraw-Hill, 1959.

Cargill, Oscar, ed. *O'Neill and His Plays: Four Decades of Criticism*. New York: New York University Press, 1961.

Carpenter, Frederic I. *Eugene O'Neill*. New York: Twayne Publishers, Inc., 1964, rev. 1979.

Chothia, Jean. *Forging a Language. A Study of the Plays of Eugene O'Neill*. Cambridge: Cambridge University Press, 1979.

Eaton, Walter Prichard. *The Theatre Guild: The First Ten Years*. New York: Scholarly Press, 1971.

Falk, Doris V. *Eugene O'Neill and the Tragic Tension: An Interpretive Study of the Plays*. New York: Gordian Press, 1982.

Floyd, Virginia. *Eugene O'Neill. A World View*. New York: Frederick Ungar, 1979.

_____, ed. *Eugene O'Neill at Work. Newly Released Ideas for Plays*. New York: Frederick Ungar, 1981.

_____. *The Plays of Eugene O'Neill: A New Assessment*. New York: Frederick Ungar, 1985.

_____, ed. *The Unfinished Plays: Notes for The Visit of Malatesta, The Last Conquest, Blind Alley Guy*. New York: Continuum, 1988.

Langner, Lawrence and Teresa Helburn. *The Story of the Theatre Guild: 1919–1947*. New York: Theatre Guild, 1947.

Leach, Clifford. *O'Neill*. New York: Barnes & Noble, Inc., 1965.

Matlaw, Myron, "Robins Hits the Road: Trouping with O'Neill in the 1880s," *Theatre Survey* 29.2 (November 1988): 175–192.

Nadel, Norman. *A Pictorial History of the Theatre Guild*. Special Material by Lawrence Langner and Armina Marshall. New York: Crown, 1969.

O'Neill, Eugene. *Eugene O'Neill to Carlotta Montgomery O'Neill*. New Haven, Conn.: Yale University Press, 1960.

_____. *More Stately Mansions*. New Haven, Conn.: Yale University Press, 1964.

_____. *Ten "Lost" Plays*. New York: Random House, 1964.

_____. *Six Short Plays*. New York: Vintage Books, 1965.

_____. *Work Diary 1924–1943*. Two volumes. Edited by Donald C. Gallup. New Haven, Conn.: Yale University Library, 1981.

_____. *The Calms of Capricorn*. Two volumes. Edited by Donald C. Gallup. New Haven, Conn.: Yale University Library, 1981.

_____. *Chris Christopherson: A Play in Three Acts*. New York: Random House, 1982.

_____. *Complete Plays*. Three volumes. Edited by Travis Bogard. New York: Viking Press, 1988.

Raleigh, John Henry. *The Plays of Eugene O'Neill*. Carbondale and Edwardsville: Southern Illinois University Press, 1965.

Shafer, Yvonne. *Performing O'Neill: Conversations with Actors and Directors*. New York: Palgrave Macmillan, 2000.

Shea, Laura, "O'Neill, the Theatre Guild, and *A Moon for the Misbegotten*," *The Eugene O'Neill Review* 27 (2005): 76–97.

Sheaffer, Louis *Eugene O'Neill: Son and Playwright.* Boston: Little, Brown and Company, 1968.

_____. *Eugene O'Neill: Son and Artist.* Boston: Little, Brown and Company, 1973.

Tornqvist, Egil. *Eugene O'Neill: A Playwright's Theatre.* Jefferson, N.C.: McFarland, 2004.

Vena, Gary, "Chipping at the Iceman: The Text and the 1946 Theatre Guild Production," *The Eugene O'Neill Newsletter* 9.3 (Winter 1985): 11–17.

Waldau, Roy S. *Vintage Years of the Theatre Guild, 1928–1939.* Cleveland, Ohio, and London: The Press of Case Western Reserve University, 1972.

Winther, Sophus K. *Eugene O'Neill: A Critical Study.* New York: Random House, 1934.

THE EDITIONS OF O'NEILL'S WORKS USED FOR THIS BOOK

O'Neill, Eugene. *O'Neill: Complete Plays 1913–1920.* New York: Library of America, 1988.

_____. *O'Neill: Complete Plays 1920–1931.* New York: Library of America, 1988.

_____. *O'Neill: Complete Plays 1932–1943.* New York: Library of America, 1988.

SOURCES CITED IN THIS BOOK

Bloom, Harold, ed. *Long Day's Journey Into Night — Eugene O'Neill. Bloom's Modern Critical Interpretations.* New York: Chelsea House Publishers, 2009.

Diggins, John Patrick. *Eugene O'Neill's America: Desire Under Democracy.* Chicago: University of Chicago Press, 2007.

O'Neill, Eugene, "Memoranda on Masks," *American Spectator,* November, 1932: 3.

Awards

"AND THE WINNER IS . . . "

Editor's Note: Eugene O'Neill was awarded the Nobel Prize in Literature in 1936.

	PULITZER PRIZE	TONY AWARD	NY DRAMA CRITICS CIRCLE AWARD		
			Best American	Best Foreign	Best Play
1918	Jesse Lynch Williams *Why Marry?*	-	-		
1919	No Award	-	-		
1920	**Eugene O'Neill** *Beyond the Horizon*	-	-		
1921	Zona Gale *Miss Lulu Bett*	-	-		
1922	**Eugene O'Neill** *"Anna Christie"*	-	-		
1923	Owen Davis *Icebound*	-	-		
1924	Hatcher Hughes *Hell-Bent Fer Heaven*	-	-		
1925	Sidney Howard *They Knew What They Wanted*	-	-		
1926	George Kelly *Craig's Wife*	-	-		
1927	Paul Green *In Abraham's Bosom*	-	-		
1928	**Eugene O'Neill** *Strange Interlude*	-	-		
1929	Elmer L. Rice *Street Scene*	-	-		
1930	Marc Connelly *The Green Pastures*	-	-		

	PULITZER PRIZE	TONY AWARD	NY DRAMA CRITICS CIRCLE AWARD		
			Best American	Best Foreign	Best Play
1931	Susan Glaspell *Alison's House*	-	-		
1932	George S. Kaufman *Of Thee I Sing*	-	-		
1933	Maxwell Anderson *Both Your Houses*	-	-		
1934	Sidney Kingsley *Men in White*	-	-		
1935	Zoe Akins *The Old Maid*	-	-		
1936	Robert E. Sherwood *Idiot's Delight*	-	Maxwell Anderson *Winterset*		
1937	Moss Hart and George S. Kaufman *You Can't Take It With You*	-	Maxwell Anderson *High Tor*		
1938	Thornton Wilder *Our Town*	-	John Steinbeck *Of Mice and Men*		
1939	Robert E. Sherwood *Abe Lincoln in Illinois*	-	No award		
1940	William Saroyan *The Time of Your Life*	-	William Saroyan *The Time of Your Life*		
1941	Robert E. Sherwood *There Shall Be No Night*	-	Lillian Hellman *Watch on the Rhine*		
1942	No Award	-	No Award		
1943	Thornton Wilder *The Skin of Our Teeth*	-	Sidney Kingsley *The Patriots*		
1944	No Award	-	No Award		
1945	Mary Chase *Harvey*	-	Tennessee Williams The Glass Managerie		
1946	Russel Crouse and Howard Lindsay *State of the Union*	-	No Award		
1947	No Award	Arthur Miller *All My Sons*	Arthur Miller *All My Sons*		
1948	Tennessee Williams *A Streetcar Named Desire*	Joshua Logan and Thomas Heggen *Mister Roberts*	Tennessee Williams *A Streetcar Named Desire*		

	PULITZER PRIZE	TONY AWARD	NY DRAMA CRITICS CIRCLE AWARD		
			Best American	Best Foreign	Best Play
1949	Arthur Miller *Death of a Salesman*	Arthur Miller *Death of a Salesman*	Arthur Miller *Death of a Salesman*		
1950	Richard Rodgers *South Pacific*	T. S. Eliot *The Cocktail Party*	Carson McCullers *A Member of the Wedding*		
1951	No Award	Tennessee Williams *The Rose Tattoo*	Sidney Kingsley *Darkness at Noon*		
1952	Joseph Kramm *The Shrike*	Jan de Hartog *The Fourposter*	John van Druten *I Am a Camera*		
1953	William Inge *Picnic*	Arthur Miller *The Crucible*	William Inge *Picnic*		
1954	John Patrick *The Teahouse of the August Moon*	John Patrick *The Teahouse of the August Moon*	John Patrick *The Teahouse of the August Moon*		
1955	Tennessee Williams *Cat on a Hot Tin Roof*	Joseph Hayes *The Desperate Hours*	Tennessee Williams *Cat on a Hot Tin Roof*		
1956	Albert Hackett and Frances Goodrich *The Diary of Anne Frank*	Albert Hackett and Frances Goodrich *The Diary of Anne Frank*	Albert Hackett and Frances Goodrich *The Diary of Anne Frank*		
1957	**Eugene O'Neill** ***Long Day's Journey Into Night***	**Eugene O'Neill** ***Long Day's Journey Into Night***	**Eugene O'Neill** ***Long Day's Journey Into Night***		

INDEX

The entries in the index include highlights from the main In an Hour essay portion of the book.

ABOUT THE AUTHOR

James Fisher, Professor of Theatre and Head of the Theatre Department at the University of North Carolina at Greensboro, has authored several books, including *Understanding Tony Kushner* (University of South Carolina Press, 2008), *The Historical Dictionary of the American Theatre: Modernism* (Scarecrow Press, 2007; co-authored with Felicia Hardison Londré), *The Theater of Tony Kushner. Living Past Hope* (NY: Routledge, 2001), *Eddie Cantor: A Bio-Bibliography* (Greenwood Press, 1997), *Spencer Tracy: A Bio-Bibliography* (Greenwood Press, 1994), *Al Jolson: A Bio-Bibliography* (Greenwood Press, 1994), and *The Theatre of Yesterday and Tomorrow: Commedia dell'Arte on the Modern Stage* (Mellen, 1992). He edited *"We Will Be Citizens": New Essays on Gay and Lesbian Drama* (McFarland, 2008), six volumes of *The Puppetry Yearbook* (Mellen Press), and *Tony Kushner: New Essays on the Art and Politics of the Plays* (McFarland, 2006). He is also a director and actor, has held several research fellowships, and is book review editor for *Broadside*, the publication of the Theatre Library Association. Fisher was 1999–2000 McLain-McTurnan-Arnold Research Scholar at Wabash College, where he taught for twenty-nine years, and he was named "Indiana Theatre Person of the Year" by the Indiana Theatre Association in 1997. In 2007, Fisher received the Betty Jean Jones Award for Excellence in the Teaching of American Theatre from the American Theatre and Drama Society.

ACKNOWLEDGMENTS

The author would like to thank his colleagues at the University of North Carolina at Greensboro, and especially his wife, Dana Warner Fisher, and their children, Daniel and Anna, for their love and support.

Know the playwright, love the play.

Open a new door to theater study, performance, and audience satisfaction with these Playwrights In an Hour titles.

ANCIENT GREEK

Aeschylus   Aristophanes   Euripides   Sophocles

RENAISSANCE

William Shakespeare

MODERN

Anton Chekhov   Noël Coward   Lorraine Hansberry
Henrik Ibsen   Arthur Miller   Molière   Eugene O'Neill
Arthur Schnitzler   George Bernard Shaw   August Strindberg
Frank Wedekind   Oscar Wilde   Thornton Wilder
Tennessee Williams

CONTEMPORARY

Edward Albee   Alan Ayckbourn   Samuel Beckett
Theresa Rebeck   Sarah Ruhl   Sam Shepard   Tom Stoppard
August Wilson

To purchase or for more information
visit our web site inanhourbooks.com